BLOOD (

MW01170815

Historic Appalachian True Crime Stories 1808-2004

R. Scott Lunsford

And

Alfred Dockery

What people are saying about Blood on the Blue Ridge.

"This book does an exceptional job of giving depth to some colorful lawbreakers while keeping with the verifiable facts." — *TnGridIronFan*

"The narrative is perfectly interspersed with facts and quotes without feeling too dense. I would recommend this book to any True Crime fan or history buff!" — *Taryn*

"Not just your run-of-the-mill crime anthology, you can tell the writers actually put in effort to research what cases they are writing about. (Also, as a librarian, the numerous sources aired at the back, chefs kiss.)" — *Kristin Chapman*

"I was impressed with the amount of detail in the book. … The chapter about the theft of artifacts from the Biltmore was most interesting as we had visited it in the early 2000s." — *Craigeri*

This is about what I'd expect from a collection of true crime stories that don't focus on a specific kind of crime. There are murders, robberies, and a bunch of other stuff. The one about rare books and the Biltmore Estate is easily my favorite from this collection. — *Matt*

Copyright

Disclaimer

The stories depicted in this book are based on newspaper articles, historical records, personal accounts, and other sources to present an accurate representation of events. While substantial effort was made to ensure the accuracy of the information, some details may be subject to interpretation, and certain events have been reconstructed based on available evidence.

The authors and publisher do not claim to provide a definitive account of any event or individual's life but endeavor to offer a thoughtful and engaging narrative based on thorough and careful research.

This book's subject matter includes descriptions of violence and other distressing topics that could be unsettling. Discretion is advised.

The authors and publisher disclaim any liability in connection with the use of this information.

For further research and more detailed information, readers are encouraged to consult the original sources and references listed at the end of the book.

The authors strive to impart an understanding and respect for the people and communities affected by these historical events

Dedication

To our spouses, Robin and Barbara, whose patience and understanding allowed us to spend the time necessary to produce a work of this quality and length. Special thanks to Barbara for tirelessly reading every version of each chapter and spotting errors that otherwise would have gone unnoticed.

To our children, who remind us that hope and redemption are always possible and sometimes likely.

To our parents, who instilled in us the values of hard work, perseverance, and fair play.

And to our friends, whose insights, stories, and willingness to share their experiences and knowledge enriched our research and made this book more than just a collection of facts.

This book is a testament to the resilience of the Appalachian people, their enduring spirit, and the constant struggle for justice.

To those who have been wronged, who have fought for fairness, and who continue to seek a brighter future, we hope this book serves as a reminder of the enduring human spirit and the pursuit of justice.

Contents

1. The Nearly Fatal Footprint

William Jackson Marion Hanging, Nebraska 1887 (Wikipedia: Public Domain).

"Never knew what hit them. Hell of a phrase, isn't it? Nothing can happen so fast that there is not a micro-instant of realization ... insofar as self-realization is concerned. We're each expert in our own death. — *John D. MacDonald, American novelist, and short story writer from his novel Cinnamon Skin.*

Suppose someone could tell you when you would die, day and time. Would you want to know? Throughout history, there have been people who knew when they were going to die. Events like the Charge of the Light Brigade in 1854 and the sinking of the RMS Titanic in 1912 come to mind. The best-known examples are, of course, condemned prisoners.

Convicted individuals who were found guilty and given the ultimate punishment of death. The time between sentencing and having the noose placed around one's neck, being strapped into the electric chair, led into the gas chamber, or strapped to a gurney for lethal injection has to be intolerable, even more so for those who are wrongfully convicted.

Reform efforts like the Innocence Project have shown us that wrongful convictions happen more often than any of us would like. Examples of wrongful convictions abound:

·   Carlos DeLuna, executed in Texas in 1989.

·   Leo Jones, executed in Florida in 1998.

·   Leonard Mack, released from a New York prison in 2023 after serving 47 years.

The historical record has a multitude of cases of judicial errors and unjust verdicts. In 1808, a set of bizarre circumstances sent Henry West to the gallows for the murder of James Craig in Buncombe County.

A Discourteous Manner and Brutal Disposition

Much of what we know about Henry West's case comes from the concise, beautifully written, and somewhat inaccurate account by renowned attorney and respected North Carolina historian F. A. Sondley (1857–1931).

From A History of Buncombe County, North Carolina:

> "'John' Craig was Buncombe County's first treasurer, then called County Trustee. In 1789, North Carolina granted him a body of land in the northeastern part of the town of Asheville, later traversed by Sunset Drive. In the latter part of his life, he resided in the eastern part of the county. There, he was shot and killed from ambush.
>
> "A personal enemy was Henry West, a sailor who had deserted from his ship at Charleston, South Carolina, and came to Buncombe. He was lame in one of his feet owing to an injury which had left a disfiguration. This

*footprint found at the place of the murder, and some
other evidence led to his being tried and convicted as a
murderer. James Patton and his sister, Mrs. Jane
Erwin, wife of Andrew Erwin, thought him innocent,
and Mrs. Erwin went to Raleigh in order to seek the
Governor's pardon, arranging for relays of horses to
bring the pardon if obtained.*

*"West conveyed a tract of land between Grassy
Branch and Bull Creek to Philip Creasman in
consideration of Creasman procuring proper burial
for West's body. Much land there and on Haw Creek
was then owned by West.*

*"The time for execution arrived. West was carried in a
wagon seated on his coffin to the place of execution, on
East and Hillside Streets now. James Patton sat beside
him. The noose was adjusted. Patton procured a little
delay by persuading the sheriff that the time fixed for
execution had not arrived. Just then, a horseman
galloped up with the pardon.*

*"West was a man of great eccentricity, much
intelligence, and quick perception but prided himself
upon a discourteous manner and brutal disposition."*

Sondley adds a couple more intriguing tidbits about West in his book
Asheville and Buncombe County:

*"Henry West was convicted of the murder but was
pardoned, the pardon arriving while he stood on the
scaffold with the sheriff ready to execute him. He was a
most eccentric character of much intelligence and
considerable property and was said to have been a
sailor and served under (John) Paul Jones in the*

Revolutionary War, but prided himself upon being discourteous in manner and brutal in disposition."

In addition to Sondley's work, we have contemporary accounts from two Raleigh newspapers: the Minerva and the Register. With help from librarians at the State Library of North Carolina, my coauthor found four petitions seeking respite (a stay of execution) or pardon for West sent to Governor Benjamin Williams in April and May of 1808. Finally, we have insights from the writings of Asheville Citizen-Times columnist Rob Neufeld and author Anne Chesky Smith.

Sondley makes a couple of errors straight out of the gate. First, it was James Craig who was murdered. In a 2019 column, Neufeld tells us that genealogists believe that James had a brother named John, which led to the confusion.

Errors of this sort are not that unusual. When my father was a boy growing up in West Asheville, he and his brother Lloyd Lunsford were riding a bike together when struck by a drunk driver. The accident killed Uncle Lloyd and put my father in the hospital. I have located several North Carolina newspaper stories with the two young men's names switched. In 1808, the newspapers did a better job, and the petitions confirmed that the murder victim was James Craig.

Second, Sondley tells us that James Craig and Henry West were enemies. It turns out West was engaged to marry Craig's daughter, so it would seem that this was not the case, but it would have led to some awkward family gatherings if true.

Shot from Ambush

An article in the April 7, 1808, Raleigh Minerva gives us some details of the crime. On Tuesday, March 15, around 4:00 p.m., James Craig was working alone at his mill beside Bull Creek, about eight miles northeast of Asheville, when his dogs began barking at something on the opposite side of the creek in a laurel thicket.

He walked over to investigate. When he got within 20 or 30 yards of the noise, a gunshot rang out from the thicket, followed by the rolling smoke of a black powder firearm. A lead ball struck him a little below his ribs and lodged just within the skin of his back.

The article goes on to tell us that Craig lived about three hours after being shot and "manifested a firm mind and retained his senses to the last moment of his life." He saw a man he believed to be his assailant run from the thicket, and he identified the man as his neighbor, Henry West.

A petition to Governor Williams dated April 20 and sent by Kyle, Hamilton et al. gives us a bit more information:

> "It appears evident on trial that the ball taken out of the body of said Craig had been shot out of a small bored rifle as the marks of the rifles and patching were plain on it. It also appeared evident that the distance he was shot was 35 yards at least; also that West neither had owned nor was in possession of a gun. Six or eight months past another person has been strongly suspected the ball of whose gun perfectly corresponded with that taken out of said Craig in weight and size ..."

The man they suspected of owning the murder weapon was Thomas Rogers, another of Craig's neighbors who had been engaged in a long and bitter lawsuit with Craig.

Given the timeframe and description of the projectile, the weapon would have most likely been a flintlock rifle of the Pennsylvania rifle or Kentucky rifle design firing a .32–.45 caliber patched round ball.

As for West's footprint, Anne Chesky Smith, in her book *Riceville*, tells us that he had an injured leg or foot that gave him a distinctive walking gait, and thus, he left distinctive footprints or tracks.

> *"A set of footprints-one shallow and one deep-were
> found at the murder scene. This evidence was used
> against West, who had a deformed leg allegedly from
> being attacked by a shark in Charleston, South
> Carolina."*

The problem with this evidence is, of course, that tracks may tell you
that someone was at a particular place, but they don't tell you when.
Depending on the medium or soil (sand, clay, or loamy) and the weather
(dry, wet, or rainy). Further, evidence placing someone at a crime scene
doesn't mean they committed the crime.

A Divided Jury

Based primarily on James Craig's dying declaration, West was arrested,
held in the Buncombe County jail, and tried on April 8-9, 24 days after
the shooting.

Page three of the April 20 petition also gives some insights into the
course of West's trial. One of the five signers was a grand jury member,
and another was a trial jury member. It states that the jury was
deadlocked with five in favor of guilty and seven in favor of not guilty.

> *"At length, his honor, Judge Locke had a Tinners
> Waggon drove up to the court house and assured the
> jury that he would have them hauled to Rutherford, the
> next court on the Circuit, and keep them together for a
> month but that they should agree."*

The petition goes on to say that the prisoner, West, was offered a mistrial
but declined because he did not want to remain in jail until the next term
of court, and the judge insinuated that this refusal was an indication of
guilt.

> *"After a few minutes retirement, the seven jurors gave up to the five and brought in the prisoner guilty. These are all facts that did and do exist."*

In the April 21st edition of the Raleigh Minerva newspaper, a one-paragraph item, reported:

> *"West was tried for the murder of Mr. James Craig on the following day - the trial was lengthy, occupying the attention of the court more than 24 hours, but on Saturday morning about ten o'clock, the jury gave in the verdict - Guilty, and Judge Locke immediately pronounced the sentence of death. He is to be executed on Friday, the 6th of May next."*

The 1808 court system moved fast. Neufeld, in his September 16, 2019, column, quotes Lucien Holt Felmet, a Harnett County attorney and a Craig descendant:

> *"This crime," Felmet stressed, "was perpetrated on March 15, the trial was held on April 8 and 9, and the execution was scheduled on May 6... What took 55 days in 1808 would consume a decade today."*

The North Carolina court system of the early 19th century was a stark contrast from the one we know today. The defendant was arrested, held for trial, and, if found guilty, received some form of corporal punishment. North Carolina did not have a prison until after the Civil War. Construction of Central Prison by inmates began in 1870. It was completed in 1884.

Thieves were flogged. Those found guilty of manslaughter had the letter M branded into the palm of their right hand. Liars and perjurers had their ears cropped. Here are two examples from John Preston Arthur's *Western North Carolina: A History (From 1730-1913)*:

*"It will be remembered that in those days, the great
terror set up before rogues was the whipping-post
where the fellow convicted of larceny got thirty-nine
lashes well laid on his bare back with long keen
switches in the hands of the sheriff."*

*"From the minutes of the County Court of Buncombe,
October 1793, it appears that it was "Ordered by court
that Thomas Hopper, upon his own motion, have a
certificate from the clerk, certifying that his right ear
was bit off by Philip Williams in a fight between said,
Hopper and Williams. Certificate issued." This was
necessary in order that the loss of a part of his ear
might not cause those ignorant of the facts to conclude
that the missing part had been removed as a
punishment for perjury or forgery."*

Your Petitioners Humbly Pray

Sondley tells us that Jane Erwin, Andrew Erwin's wife, went to Raleigh
to seek a pardon for West, arranging for relays of horses to bring the
pardon if obtained. We have no way of knowing if the horse relay
actually took place, but it would have been a good idea. The 250-mile
journey from Raleigh to Asheville would have taken days.

The only way a message or document from the governor could reach
Asheville was by horseback or horse-powered conveyance. The
telegraph came to Asheville on July 28, 1877. The first train pulled into
Asheville from Salisbury on October 3, 1880.

As for who traveled to Raleigh to persuade Governor Williams to
intervene, the most likely candidate was Hamilton Kyle, a member of the
grand jury that indicted West.

According to an item dated May 5 in the Raleigh Register, a member of
the grand jury traveled to Raleigh to lobby the governor for a stay of

execution for West to allow for further investigation of the crime. From the article:

> *"He procured a petition from a few of his neighbors, & at his own expense, set out for this city, in order to lay the case before the Governor,"*

Kyle not only wrote G. (grand) Juror next to his signature in the April 20 Kyle, Hamilton et al. petition, but he is named as the bearer of a letter sent by Andrew Erwin, who also signed that petition.

In the letter, Erwin says that the Kyle brothers, it appears that one was on the grand jury, and the other was on West's trial jury, could make the case for West better than Erwin could in a letter.

In a strange twist, Erwin discloses that they deliberately kept the petition a secret from West. From the letter:

> *"We could have procured a much greater number of signers to the petition had we have risked letting West know any petition of any kind had gone forward that in order that he may make a confession should it still be possible that he is guilty. We are determined to keep the result of the petition an entire secret from him."*

They believed Henry West to be innocent and were aware of new evidence that pointed to another suspect, and yet they kept the possibility of pardon from him that he might confess on the gallows if he was guilty. It's a mindset that is difficult to grasp in the 21st century.

A Declaration on the Gallows

If done correctly, a hanging is supposed to be a quick and relatively painless death. However, if the rope is too short, the noose will slowly strangle the condemned. If the rope was too long, it could pull the head free of the body. Multiple methods evolved over time, including the short drop, pole method, standard drop, and long drop.

The goal is to cause a severe subluxation of the C2 and C3 vertebrae or "hangman's fracture" that crushes the spinal cord and disrupts the vertebral arteries.

Unfortunately for West, before 1850, the short drop was the standard method of hanging; it killed by strangulation.

May 6 arrived, and West was conveyed to the scaffold. He climbed steps and, standing on the trap with the rope around his neck and the sheriff beside him, West declared: "I had no part in the murder of Craig, either in thought, word, or action."

Fortunately for all concerned, a rider arrived with a letter from the governor granting a respite until June 3. If James Patton really was present, fiddling with his pocket watch and arguing with the sheriff about whether or not it was indeed noon, then he saved West's life along with the Kyles and Andrew Erwin.

From the Thursday, May 26, 1808, Raleigh Minerva:

> *"Since the suspension of execution, petitions from most of the respectable men of that county, including the whole of the petit jury, but one who was absent, have been presented to Governor Williams, praying a pardon of West, which we are happy to state has been granted.*

> *"The petitioners express their belief, from what has transpired since the trial of West, of his innocence. Indeed, it would appear unlikely that he should have perpetrated the murder, as he was at the time engaged to be married to the daughter of the deceased and to whom it is yet believed, will be married."*

Epilogue

Frustratingly, neither Henry West nor Thomas Rogers turn up again in any newspapers or documents we could find. We cannot tell you if West went on to marry Craig's daughter or if Rogers was tried for the murder, and if so, whether he was found guilty or not guilty.

All we can say for certain is that West dodged the gallows because concerned citizens and jurors made an impressive effort, which included hand-carrying a petition to Raleigh, and because Governor Williams granted him respite that arrived barely in the nick of time.

Should this be a lesson for today? The strength and validity of our criminal justice system depend on its accuracy — its ability to convict the guilty and to clear the innocent. Yet, we know that wrongful convictions happen.

(Editor's Note: Several sources incorrectly state that David Stone was governor during West's trial and near execution. Stone was elected governor in 1808 but was sworn in on 12 December 1808. Today N.C. governors take office in January. The Thursday, May 26, 1808, Raleigh Minerva is incorrectly indexed as the Tuesday, April 26, 1808, Raleigh Minerva on newspapers.com.)

2. The Hermit of Bald Mountain

The Trappers' Last Shot by William Tylee Ranney 1850 (LOC: Public Domain).

"A fine line separates the weary recluse from the fearful hermit. Finer still is the line between hermit and bitter misanthrope." — Dean Koontz, American Writer, from his novel Velocity.

In November 1824, the U.S. presidential election was still undecided because none of the four candidates, John Quincy Adams, Henry Clay, William Crawford, or Andrew Jackson, had won a majority of the Electoral College. As part of his year-long tour of the United States, the 67-year-old Marquis de Lafayette, the only surviving major general of the American Revolutionary War, visited Thomas Jefferson in Virginia. Constable William Erwin and his assistant, James Cooper, were escorting a prisoner named Higgins to the Justice of the Peace in Jonesborough, TN.

While Adams went on to become the 6th president of the United States and Lafayette made it safely back to France aboard the frigate USS Brandywine, Higgins never saw Jonesborough alive.

A concealed rifleman fired on Erwin and his party but missed. If the constable thought the worst was behind them, he was mistaken. The shooter managed to get ahead of them and fired again, this time from an outhouse (some accounts suggest it was an abandoned cabin). His aim was true. Higgins was hit in the chest near his collarbone and died on the spot.

When Erwin saw his prisoner fall, he sprinted to the structure and threw open the door. Inside, he found a large man armed with a flintlock rifle and an ax. Undeterred, Erwin came to grips with the man.

A violent scuffle ensued. The man attempted to bring his rifle to bear, but his size and the low joists of the privy prevented him from maneuvering it clear. He then strove to get hold of his other weapon. Erwin had none of it and smacked him across the head with a wooden cudgel, knocking the big man to his knees. The man stood up. Erwin clubbed him again, harder this time. Again, the man went to his knees and rose.

Sensing that the issue was in doubt, Erwin ordered Cooper to shoot the man. Cooper complied, hitting the giant in the hand. The wound took enough of the fight out of him for Erwin and Cooper to secure him, and they arrested David Greer, known to history as the Hermit of Bald Mountain, for the murder of Holland Higgins.

The details about Higgins's death and Greer's hard-fought capture come from a January 1825 article in the American Economist and East Tennessee Statesman, published in Greeneville 1822–1826. Multiple other papers reprinted the article, crediting it to either the Greenville Economist or the Tennessee Statesman, including the Charleston, S.C., Daily Courier; Lexington, KY, Gazette; and Pennsylvania Republican (York, PA).

Another startling record of the crime is Higgins' headstone in Erwin, TN, which bears the legend "Shot and killed by David Greer Nov. 30, 1824."

The London Morning Chronicle was one of the papers that reprinted the article from the Economist, making it an international story. The article ran under the column heading "Horrid Murder" alongside items about a levy for British regiments in India and news of a fire in Dublin, Ireland. Greer was now famous or infamous. The article also ran in the North Devon Journal-Herald, about 180 miles southwest of London.

Murder Trial and a "Deranged" Verdict

Greer was tried in the March 1825 term of the circuit court in Jonesborough. At the end of the two-day trial, the jury returned a verdict of acquittal in consequence of insanity. A bond was given to the court for the prisoner to keep the peace for one year, and he was set free. One wonders if they gave him his rifle and ax back.

The Greeneville paper covered the trial, and the account was even more widely shared than the earlier report of the crime itself, at least in the United States. We found the article in newspapers from Alabama, Connecticut, Delaware, Maine, Maryland, Pennsylvania, South Carolina, Vermont, and Virginia.

The article begins with the Greeneville paper's admission that it did not have a reporter present at the trial but had collected "some of the prominent incidents from a conversation with a gentleman who was present during the greater part of it and here give them to our readers."

The article is an exciting mix of fact and speculation. It states that Greer and Higgins got into a fistfight over a disagreement in their trading, and Greer had Higgins arrested "for the sole purpose of having a good chance to shoot him while he was under arrest." It also mentions that Greer wrote his own constitution for a government, which was introduced at trial as evidence of his "lunacy."

The report goes on to say that Greer left civilization and settled on Bald Mountain due to the unhappy termination of a "love affair," where he had spent the last 20 or more years on or near the mountaintop. He protested a tax that the court of Buncombe County levied on him with spectacular violence, yet he was very kind to visitors who came to see "the strange man of the mountain." Greer also grew potatoes and corn on the mountaintop, protecting them with a ditch. He later moved this garden downslope because the growing season was too short at Big Bald's highest point, 5,516 feet (1,681 m) above sea level.

Among the less well-documented and perhaps less credible claims made in the article are that Greer rented cattle grazing rights on the top of the bald and even had it marked off into patches: "Hazle Patch, Haw Thicket, &c. &c." He built a small gristmill "kept in motion by the water of a small mountain stream." It could grind a half bushel to a bushel of grain per day. He was also credited with building an "iron manufactory" on the mountain. He had uncommon physical strength, demonstrated by his single-handed construction of the mill and other machinery.

Perhaps the most outlandish claim the paper made was that he was Turkish on his father's side. The surname Greer is usually associated with Scotland. Later reports suggested that he may have been German. An article in a Knoxville newspaper said he was a "Polander."

The Frontier Between Fact and Folklore

Each newspaper reporter or book author had a different take on the hermit and added or subtracted details to the story. Just as Greer went into the wilderness to find comfort for his broken heart, let's set out and explore the story of the Hermit of Bald Mountain.

Let's start with the facts of David Greer's life, on which most of the writers agree. Greer, a South Carolina native, came to work for David Vance near current-day Weaverville, N.C., around 1798 and fell hopelessly in love with one of his daughters. By all accounts, Greer was well educated for the day, strong, and a hard worker. Three years later, when the young lady married another man, he was devastated and, a few days later, set out to find a home far from civilization with only a rifle, a knapsack, and $250 in back wages. He settled on Big Bald Mountain, apparently stopped in his tracks by the sublime view from its summit.

A bit of background on the Vance family: Colonel David Vance, Sr., served in the U.S. Revolutionary War at the battles of Brandywine, Germantown, and Valley Forge. He also took part in the battles of Musgrove Mill and Kings Mountain. He was the grandfather of Zebulon Vance, N.C. governor, U.S. senator, and Confederate officer. Greer was most likely smitten with Jane Vance, who married Hugh Davidson, or possibly Sarah Vance, who married Charles McLean.

There are several accounts of Greer traveling to a courthouse after being told he was required to pay a 75-cent poll tax. Two of these specifically mention Buncombe County or Asheville. All of them say he showed up with a rifle in hand and threw rocks, breaking the windows and pelting everyone present, the judge, jury, lawyers, and sheriff, until he drove them from the building.

Given how early and often the claim is made, it seems likely true. At the same time, it's hard to believe that one man armed with a flintlock could raise that much havoc without being arrested. We're giving this one a 50/50 chance of being factual.

Ditches and Graves

One of the most tantalizing details of the hermit's story is the ditch he dug on the mountain. Its location, dimensions, and purpose vary depending on the account or author. The article about Greer's trial described the ditch as a means to secure his mountaintop potato and corn patches from intrusion, most likely from rabbits, deer, groundhogs, and raccoons.

According to an 1838 newspaper article at that time, the ditch was still visible and was originally dug eight feet deep without hitting either rock or clay in a spacious field on the summit. Unfortunately, the report does not state the ditch's purpose.

Pat Alderman in *Wonders of the Unakas Unicoi County* says Greer dug a ditch four feet deep and four feet wide as a moat to keep his livestock in and other people's stock out. Both of Alderman's books have a photo of a person kneeling in a depression on the Bald's summit, which is described as the remains of the four-by-four ditch "dug as a fence." In *Greasy Cove in Unicoi County*, he refers to it as an "animal barrier."

In his book *Two Worlds in the Tennessee Mountains*, David Hsiung quotes David A. Deaderick's diary, which describes Greer's ditch work on the mountain as being on "the pinnacle of which he had ditched for the purpose of cultivation."

Another compelling question about the hermit is why he killed Higgins. The earliest newspaper articles do not mention a motive. An 1838 article reports that Higgins lied to Greer, which was the one offense he would not tolerate. Lanman wrote in 1849 that Higgins was killed for hunting deer on Greer's property. Zeigler & Grosscup, writing in 1883, say it was over real or imaginary land rights. Alderman tells us that he killed Higgins to acquire a cherry orchard adjacent to his property. Hsiung stated in 1997 that Higgins encroached on Greer's land.

While there is some debate over exactly where and when it happened, most sources agree that George Tompkins, a blacksmith whom Greer had threatened to kill, shot and killed Greer in 1834. Greer was buried in an unmarked grave, and Tomkins was never tried for the shooting due to Greer's reputation for violently carrying out his threats.

Trailing the Hermit Through Time

We know much about Greer's life and exploits, even though a significant portion of the story cannot be true. The first written mention of Greer is in newspapers from 1825. The articles cover Greer's murder of Higgins and his subsequent trial, as discussed above.

The hermit's story was carried forward in newspapers and books. Interest in David Greer rose and fell over the decades, with a big surge in the 1970s, probably due to the writings of Pat Alderman. While the details of his life vary from the likely to the preposterous, this romantic, mysterious, and sometimes terrifying figure continues to captivate an audience even today.

In 1849, Charles Lanman, a newspaper editor, librarian, and private secretary to Senator Daniel Webster, told the hermit's story in his book *Letters from the Alleghany Mountains*.

Lanman described Greer as a "literary recluse" who wrote singular works on religion and human government. He paints a dark portrait of the hermit, saying that he mutilated cattle that strayed onto his property and used his rifle to shoot down on the plantations of his neighbors.

In 1883, Wilber Zeigler and Ben Grosscup, two Ohio lawyers who traveled through North Carolina to research their jointly written book, *The Heart of the Alleghanies or Western North Carolina*, refer to the hermit as David Grier and credit the "posthumous papers of Silas McDowell" for the "facts of the hermit's singular history." McDowell was a science-based apple orchardist and writer from Franklin, N.C.

Zeigler and Grosscup tell us that Greer built a permanent lodge in one of the mountain's coves and cleared a nine-acre tract. He subsisted by hunting and using a portion of the $250 paid to him by Colonel Vance for his services. They also say that Greer published a pamphlet justifying his actions after his trial and sold it on the streets. If only that pamphlet had survived to the present day.

In 1914, John Preston Arthur, secretary of the Street Railway Co. in Asheville, who later became company manager and superintendent, quoted Zeigler's and Grosscup's account in his book, Western North Carolina: A History (1730–1913), passing the hermit's tale forward into the 20th century.

Arthur, writing under the pen name Bud Wuntz for the Raleigh Morning Post, mentioned David Greer in one of his 1903 columns. He described Greer as a "demented hermit." In the column, Arthur said that after he killed Higgins, Greer was killed on his first trip to "Irving" (most likely Erwin, TN) to buy coffee and ammunition.

Arthur/Wuntz concluded the Greer portion of the column with: "One of the descendants of the murdered Higgins told me this story, and I have no doubt of its truth. Those were wild, rough times, and human life was held cheap."

Pat Alderman, a choir director and writer who lived in Erwin, wrote two books, *Wonders of the Unakas in Unicoi County* and *Greasy Cove in Unicoi County*, in the 1960s and 1970s, which included stories about the hermit.

Alderman is the first source to say the hermit was called "Hog Greer" and that local mothers would use stories about him to scare their children. His work is also the source of what my co-writer and I have come to call "the hat trick." Most sources agree that Greer was killed by a blacksmith named Tompkins, who, when threatened by Greer, took the law into his own hands and shot first. Details vary on exactly when, where, and how Greer's demise happened.

In Alderman's version, Greer, angry that the blacksmith did not have his tools ready on time, left the shop and immediately set up a blind to ambush the blacksmith when he left work for the day. A neighbor who happened to be in the shop placed Tompkins's hat on a "gun stick" and held it up to a window. The hat was instantly shot off the stick. The blacksmith scrounged around the shop to find a bullet and powder to load his rifle, stuck it out a window, and shot Greer in the back as he rose from the blind.

Lanman's version, in which Tompkins went armed after being threatened and encountered Greer on the road with a rifle in hand and shot first, seems much more likely.

In 1976, Greer shared the front page of the Asheville Citizen-Times with Patty Hearst, the famous newspaper heiress on trial for her involvement with the Symbionese Liberation Army, when the legendary newspaper columnist and folklorist John Parris introduced a new generation of readers to the hermit of Bald Mountain and compared Greer to Lochinvar, the fictional romantic hero of the ballad "Marmion" by Sir Walter Scott, in his Roaming the Mountains column.

Alas, unlike Lochinvar, who arrived unannounced to his beloved's wedding, danced her out the door, and spirited her away, Greer could only watch his beloved marry another and then flee into the wilderness and a tragic existence.

3. The Unconquerable Nancy Franklin

The Colonel Allen House, Marshall, N.C., was ransacked by Union sympathizers from Laurel in 1863. Photo by Warren LeMay (Flickr: Public Domain).

"The real war will never get in the books." — *Walt Whitman, American poet, essayist, and journalist.*

"Nancy Franklin is perhaps one of the most remarkable women of the war. If one-half of the stories told about her are true, she must have been a real heroine," said M. E. Weeks, pension examiner, in his February 17, 1875, letter to James H. Baker, Commissioner of Pensions. There can be no question raised as to her loyalty to the Union during all the war. After her three sons were murdered, she became desperate and was one of the most efficient spies in the whole Union Army. She is a thoroughly immoral woman, however, and is certainly a hard case."

Nancy Franklin always had a challenging time of it. She lived in a remote mountainous corner of North Carolina. She survived at least six childbirths and an unknowable number of injuries and illnesses at a time when a poor harvest, a bad winter, or a combination of both could prove deadly to a person, family, or even a community.

She was born Nancy Shelton in 1825 in the White Rock community of Shelton Laurel in what is now Madison County. Her parents were Roderick Shelton and Rachel Moore Shelton. She was the third of 10 children. She would lose multiple family members at the Shelton Laurel massacre in 1863; more on that later.

Her story has been told many times in books and newspaper articles. Unfortunately, many, if not most, of these accounts get critical details of her story wrong. In this chapter, we will work to piece together a more accurate version of Nancy's story. It's the story of a strong, tough, and sometimes violent woman who weathered a time when chaos and horror roamed freely through the region.

The Murder of Drury Norton

Nancy married Drury Norton sometime around 1840, at 16, and over the next decade, gave birth to two daughters and four sons: Catherine, Balis, James, George, Josiah, and Delana.

In May of 1854, a brawl led to Drury's death. We have some details of the incident from N.C. Supreme Court records. Drury had been working some new ground with his father-in-law Roderick Shelton and brother-in-law Lewis Shelton. The record states that Norton "had drunk freely in the morning, but after his day's work and eating his dinner (lunch), he had become sober."

When he got home from the field, he found another brother-in-law, James Shelton, and Shelton's friend, Tilman Landers, waiting there.

Some words passed between the men, and Landers spit tobacco juice in Norton's eyes, and Norton threw liquor in his face. Then James Shelton threw him out of the door. Norton picked up a maul (basically a wooden sledgehammer), and Shelton jumped over a fence and came up with an axe. Norton jumped into the house through a window; Shelton struck at him with the axe but hit the window facing instead; after this, they threw stones at each other.

At this point, Norton threatened to go and get a warrant. He traveled a half-mile to the house of his neighbor, Gunter, and asked to borrow a gun, but the man refused. Norton returned home; as a precaution, he went through the orchard. It was here that someone struck him on the head, most likely with a rock. He was found attempting to crawl home. Norton's skull was fractured. He died three days later on a Sunday.

James Shelton and Tilman Landers fled to Tennessee. Governor David Reid offered a $200 reward for Shelton and $150 for Landers. We could find no details of their capture, but they were tried in Buncombe County in April 1855. James Shelton was found guilty of murder and Landers of manslaughter. Shelton appealed, and the N.C. Supreme Court reversed the decision because the only witness to the fatal blow was the deceased, who could not be cross-examined. Shelton lived to be 80. Tilman Landers only reached 40 and appears to have served in both Confederate and Union armies.

Nancy was left to tend a farm and provide for six children, ranging in age from three to 13 years old. The emotional trauma of seeing her husband attacked, chased, and dying slowly from a fractured skull must have been extreme.

On March 7, 1857, she married George Franklin. It would be a troubled relationship. Reports say that George was a poor provider, a drinker, and consorted with other women. In an 1883 deposition, Nancy's son, George Norton, stated that George Franklin "never has been stout."

The June 24, 1869, Asheville News has a brief item about the case of State vs. Nancy Franklin for stabbing a woman named Susan in a fit of jealousy the previous fall. It goes on to note: "The wound inflicted was a severe one, and for a while, the life of the injured woman was thought to be in danger."

Nadia Dean, in *Murder in the Mountains*, notes that Nancy was also charged with assaulting a woman named Mary Wilson in 1866 and attacked a third woman in 1870. The couple divorced around 1876.

The Shelton Laurel Massacre

The next traumatic event in Nancy Franklin's life would be as historic as it was tragic: the Shelton Laurel Massacre. According to Dean, Nancy lost six kinsmen in the Shelton Laurel massacre. She may have even witnessed the shooting or been involved in retrieving the victims' bodies from a shallow trench in which they were hastily and haphazardly buried and helping rebury them. One way or another, she lived through its aftermath.

A Confederate regiment led by Lieutenant Colonel James A. Keith executed 13 men and boys, ages 13 to 60, who were suspected of participating in the Marshall Salt raid and being Union sympathizers. Several Shelton Laurel women, young and old, were tortured to extract information about their sons' and husbands' whereabouts. It was one of the most horrific crimes of the war.

From the July 15, 1863, Memphis Bulletin report on the massacre:

> *"Old Mrs. Sallie Moore, seventy years of age, was whipped with hickory rods till the blood ran in streams down her back to the ground, and the perpetrators of this were clothed in the habiliments of rebellion and bore the name of soldiers!"*

The massacre was in retaliation for the looting of salt stores in nearby Marshall and the ransacking of Lt. Colonel Allen's home. His two children were sick with scarlet fever and died a few days later. Many feel that his children's death may have been a factor in the maltreatment handed out to the people of Laurel. The Confederate government had been hoarding salt, essential for preserving meat to get through the winter. They went so far as to place the salt in depots and guard it with troops.

From "Atrocity at Shelton Laurel" by Philip Gerard in Our State magazine:

> *"Brigadier General W.G.M. Davis reports on February 2, "I think the attack on Marshall was gotten up to obtain salt, for want of which there is great suffering in the mountains. Plunder of other property followed as a matter of course."*

The Laurel Raid

Ten years after watching her first husband die and less than two years after losing family members in one of the worst war crimes of the Civil War, on September 27, 1864, Nancy Franklin experienced the worst day of her life.

All four of her sons were home from the war. George and James were on leave from the 2nd Regiment, Company E, North Carolina Mounted Infantry (Union) from Bulls Gap, TN. Balis was also in Company E of the 2nd, but it is unclear if he was on leave. Even his brother George could not say for sure in an 1883 deposition. Josiah had been a member of the 3rd Regiment, North Carolina Mounted Infantry (Union) but had been captured in a recent raid on Strawberry Plains, TN, by Confederates and given parole due to his youth.

(Editor's Note: My great uncle, Alfred Lemuel Dockery, was a sergeant in Company C of the 2nd North Carolina Mounted Infantry. - AD)

The April 20, 1886, House Report on Nancy Franklin (No. 1793) summarizes the raid on the Franklin farm as follows:

"The evidence shows that the three sons were at home on a short furlough. They were about getting breakfast in the morning; the house was surrounded by the rebels; the boys ran out of the house … Bayliss and Josiah were shot down by the rebels. James was shot down some distance from the house. They were buried in one grave without a coffin. The house was also burned down."

Confederate Major Charles M. Roberts, 14th NC Battalion Cavalry, was mortally wounded in the engagement and died two days later. Even badly outnumbered and taken by surprise, the Norton boys extracted a toll from their attackers. George Norton, in his 1883 deposition, estimated the rebel force at about 140 men.

"I was at one of my uncles, about 3 miles away from the scene of their death, but I suppose it was not more than 2 hours after the shooting that I came over and saw them dead – all them," said George Norton.

From the October 11, 1864, Charlotte Democrat newspaper:

> *"We are pained to learn that Maj. Charles M. Roberts, of the 14th Battalion, was severely wounded last Tuesday (September 27) on Laurel while leading a party of his men against some bushwhackers who had taken refuge in a house. Maj. Roberts died last night, at 9 o'clock. No truer or braver man has fallen in this war. We trust an able pen will do justice to his memory - Asheville News, (Sept.) 29th."*

Other written works, including several books, offer a far more detailed account of the raid on the Franklin farm and its aftermath, but do they provide accurate details, or are they just myths refined by a century of circulation? One thing we have learned in our journey writing about historical crimes is that what you write about an event or incident usually comes down to what you can document. What if you don't have documentation and you elect to rely on "the story widely told today?"

Well, that's what science fiction and fantasy writer Manly Wade Wellman did in this 1956 story, "With Your Teeth in a Throat!" published by the Raleigh News and Observer. The story got the entire front page in Section III of the Sunday paper and featured vivid illustrations by N&O staff artist Bill Ballard.

The problem is the oral accounts he relied on were wrong.

Wellman's most egregious errors, which he repeated in his book, *The Kingdom of Madison: A Southern Mountain Fastness And Its People*, published almost two decades later, was claiming that Nancy Franklin and her sons were Confederate sympathizers and that their farm was attacked by a detachment of Union troops, and telling the story of a shooting at Mars Hill College that almost certainly never happened. There is also a score of minor errors in his work, including getting the names of Nancy's sons wrong.

The Myth of the Murdered Mason

This brings us to the myth of the murdered mason, which supposedly happened in 1867 at Mars Hill College. According to the story, Mars Hill College was rebuilding after the war, and workmen, particularly brick masons, came from far and wide. One of these bricklayers had been one of the "Yankees" that Wellman claims Nancy Franklin told her boys to "run off." But Nancy's sons were Union soldiers, and her farm was raided by Confederate troops.

This particular raider had shot at Nancy point-blank, and the bullet had cut off a lock of her hair. He bragged about missing this seemingly easy shot to his coworkers, and some students overheard the tale and brought it to the attention of Nancy's brother, who she was living with at the time, James Norton. But while Nancy had a brother named James, his last name was Shelton. Also, Nancy and James may not have been on the best of terms after Drury Norton's murder.

"James Norton" gave one of the students a five-dollar gold piece to point the man out and traveled with him to Mars Hill. There, he confronted the raider, "brought out a long-barrelled revolver," and shot the brick mason in front of a dozen witnesses and then hurried away. The mason died three days later.

Eventually, the killer was captured and jailed in Marshall, where "One legend says that he was cheered for hours outside the barred windows." But no one wrote about it. The prosecutor managed to get a change of venue to Burnsville in Yancy County. However, researchers have not to date found a record of the trial.

Interestingly, when James Shelton killed Drury Norton in a deserted orchard in 1854, there was a story in the newspapers within days and a reward offered for his capture within weeks. When he and Landers were tried for the killing, additional reports were published. However, we have not found any contemporary newspaper articles about a shooting in broad daylight in Mars Hill for which we are told there were eyewitnesses or articles about or records of the Burnsville trial.

The story goes on to say that when James Norton was tried in Burnsville. Nancy Franklin saddled a gray mare and rode twenty miles to testify on her brother's behalf. (White Rock to Burnsville is 20 miles traveling in a direct line, which, as anyone who has ever been to Madison or Yancy county will tell you, is impossible, and 40 miles using roads.) Her testimony was so heartfelt and moving that grown men cried, and the jury acquitted the defendant even though it was clear he was guilty.

According to Wellman's article, Judge James L. Henry interrupted her recital with a shocked question.

> *"Madam," he said, "you tell us that you told these young boys, one of them not much more than a child, to open fire and kill those men. How could you do that? Didn't you tell them to live law-abiding, Christian lives?"*

*"Yes, Your Honor," she flashed back. "I told them to
live law-abiding, Christian lives. I brought them up, to
tell the truth and be honest. But I also told them if you
have to die, die like a damned dog with your teeth in a
throat!"*

However, Dan Slagle's research indicates that James L. Henry did not
become a judge until 1868. And no contemporary newspaper reporter
took down and published this immortal quote.

Since the time Wellman wrote the article and book, many documents
have surfaced that contradict the story he was told. Unfortunately,
Wellman's book has been used by several authors as a documented
source to continue this historical game of telephone.

C. Beale Fletcher's 1959 article "Revenge Dear for Nancy Norton" in the
Asheville Citizen-Times correctly identifies Nancy and her sons as pro-
Union but repeats most of Wellman's other mistakes.

Paludan's 1981 book Victims: *A True Story of The Civil War* repeats the
story of the Mars Hill killing and cites Wellman as the source. Ironically,
on the same page, Paludan chronicles James Shelton's and Tilman
Lander's assault on Drury Norton, never realizing that Drury Norton was
Nancy Franklin's first husband and that James Shelton was her brother.
Trotter's 1988 book *Bushwhackers* has the Norton boys as Confederates
and repeats the story of the mason's fate. Inscoe and McKinney, in their
2003 book, *The Heart of Confederate Appalachia*: Western North
Carolina in the Civil War, make this passing reference:

*"In Madison County, a laborer working on a
construction project at Mars Hill College bragged to
fellow workers about his role as part of a home guard
unit that had murdered three brothers and nearly
killed their mother. Days later, the mother's brother,
James Norton, approached the work site in broad
daylight, announced his relationship to the laborer's*

victims, and shot the man. Norton was tried for murder but acquitted."

The myth of the murdered mason is a story with no documented foundation that will live forever.

Epilogue

For more than 20 years, Nancy Franklin doggedly pursued a pension as a dependent of her murdered sons. In 1886, she finally got it when the bill (H. R. 7365) for the relief of Nancy Franklin was passed. Nancy Franklin died on January 5, 1903, in Greene County, TN, at 78.

While C. Beale Fletcher's 1959 newspaper story got about as much wrong as right, the legendary dancer, dance instructor, and author of instructional dance books did perhaps the best job of summing up at least a decade (1854–1864) of Nancy Franklin's life in one sentence.

"The only moral to this story is that violence begets violence and that if you lived in Shelton Laurel, North Madison County, during the Civil War, you couldn't win for losing!"

We'll cut him some slack on the article's title, "Revenge Dear for Nancy Norton." Editors wrote the headlines back then. Unfortunately, it implies that Nancy's desire for revenge led to her sons' deaths. It's not clear that she was at home when her farm was attacked, and it seems unlikely she would have directed her three sons to chase off 140 attackers. Whether she ever suggested that they "die like dogs with their teeth in a throat," it seems unlikely anyone on Laurel would have surrendered after the Shelton Laurel massacre less than two years prior.

Everything Nancy Franklin ever had cost her dearly. Her first husband was clubbed to death with a rock and died over a period of days. She and her second husband had irreconcilable differences. She lived through the terror of the Shelton Laurel massacre, losing multiple family members. She lost three sons, ages 21, 19, and 15, and had her house burned down all in one day. But somehow, she found a way to continue both during the war and after. She was unconquerable.

(Editor's Note: We are indebted to Dan Slagle for making available to us multiple documents that we would not have otherwise had access to. We could not have told this story as accurately or as well without his assistance.)

4. Thomas Strange: Wealth, Power, and a Murder in Appalachia

Stagecoach Circa 1900-1910 (LOC: Public Domain).

"Nobody's ever been arrested for a murder; they have only ever been arrested for not planning it properly." — Terry Hayes, English screenwriter, producer, and author, from I Am Pilgrim.

A dispute between a hot-headed young Eastern scion and a proud, stubborn mountaineer led to a deadly shooting and a trial that kept an entire state spellbound. A change of venue, a dozen high-dollar defense attorneys, and a judge known for questionable rulings and ignorance of the law led to the defendant going free. For decades, the incident, trial, and acquittal would foster outrage throughout Western North Carolina.

In August 1875, a group of seven well-heeled young men from Eastern North Carolina, including Thomas W. Strange, 20, and Preston L. Bridgers, 19, took a pleasure trip through the Carolina mountains.

Thursday, August 19th found them in Waynesville, NC, about 30 miles southwest of Asheville, where they hired wagons to take them to Cataloochee Falls to do some fishing and sightseeing.

They planned to leave the Smathers Hotel in Waynesville at 7 a.m., but one of the wagons was late. When James A. Murray arrived with the wagon, it was almost 10 a.m. Thomas Strange asked him why he was so late. Murray responded that he had to shoe some horses that morning.

Strange said this was no excuse because five hours' notice had been given the day before. Murray said he had not been given that notice, and anyone who said otherwise was a liar. Strange wanted to know if Murray's ungentlemanly language was meant for him. Murray said that it was, and he offered to whip Strange or any two members of his party. Strange picked up a chair off the hotel porch and attempted to hit Murray with it.

The two men were separated, tempers were allowed to cool, and the travelers, along with their baggage, were loaded into Murray's wagon and a hack operated by a Black man named Stephen, and the excursion was at last on its way.

Strange was unwilling or unable to let the matter drop. As he got into the wagon, his fellow travelers heard him say he would settle this hereafter. They stopped at a mill just outside town to pick up Bridgers' and Strange's baggage. Having traveled separately from Asheville to Waynesville, they had stored their luggage there. Again, Strange said he wanted to settle the matter.

One of his companions, John D. Williams, Jr., said to him, "Pshaw, get your baggage and let us go fishing."

Unfortunately, neither Williams nor any of the rest of his party would get a chance to do any fishing on this trip, but in eight months, they would have a reunion of sorts as most of them were called as witnesses when Thomas Strange was tried for first-degree murder.

A Broken Wheel, A Game of Cards, and A Shooting

The group stopped 10 miles outside town to have lunch at Boyd's store. They invited Murray to eat with them, and no one mentioned the morning's disturbance. Three miles further on, the hack broke a wheel. Stephen was dispatched to find a replacement. Murray provided cushions and blankets. Most of the party passed the time playing Euchre, a popular card game of the period.

Strange borrowed a Smith & Wesson revolver from Bridgers and left the group to walk down to the wagon where Murray was sitting. Some witnesses said they did not see Bridgers give him the pistol. Bridgers testified that Strange asked for the pistol, and he gave it to him, saying, "Don't shoot away my cartridges, Tom; I don't have many."

A few moments later, they heard a gunshot followed by a scream. The group moved in the direction of the sounds and saw Murray coming toward them with one hand on his mouth and the other on his chest. He fell to the ground and died moments later without saying a word. They saw Strange walking up the road a short distance behind Murray.

Multiple witnesses testified they heard Strange say he shot Murray and that he did it in self-defense. W. H. Pemberton's testimony, as quoted by the May 4, Asheville Citizen:

> *"Here I am, gentlemen," Strange said. "I shot him in self-defense. I went there to have a quiet conversation with him and to get him to retract his remark of this morning. He advanced upon me with his knife, and I shot him in self-defense."*

Dr. H. M. Rogers, who examined Murray's body the next day, testified that the ball (or bullet) entered the left breast just under the collarbone, ranged diagonally across to the right and slightly downward. The grand jury indictment further described it as "one mortal wound to the depth of four inches and of the breadth of half an inch."

None of Strange's companions testified to seeing or finding Murray's knife. At trial, J.C. Leatherwood, a magistrate, testified that when he examined Murray's body using a lamp at the crime scene about 10:00 p.m., he found Murray's knife closed in the man's right pants pocket.

It is impossible to know what happened in the confrontation, but it seems more than coincidental that Strange shot Murray immediately after borrowing a revolver from Bridgers. If his motive was to get Murray to apologize, why didn't he take Bridgers with him? Then, he would have had both a witness and a gun.

Looking at the situation from Murray's point of view, it seems unlikely that he would attempt to stab Strange. Murray was reported to be 30 pounds heavier than Strange and a man accustomed to hard physical labor. He could have easily bested Strange with his fists as he offered to do in Waynesville.

Further, not only was Murray outnumbered six to one by his passengers, but according to Bridgers' trial testimony, the travelers had five pistols, two shotguns, and a rifle between them. Murray was also well aware of the class difference between himself and his passengers; stabbing any of them would have likely earned him a trip to prison or the gallows. Finally, would Strange have shot a man coming at him with a knife only once?

Family Connections and Legal Legacies

Early newspaper reports were quick to point out Strange's and Bridgers' family connections. Strange was the son of Colonel Robert W. Strange, a lawyer and former aide to Confederate General Braxton Bragg, and grandson of the late Judge Robert Strange, who had been a US Senator. Bridgers was the son of Robert Rufus Bridgers, a former Confederate congressman, lawyer, banker, and president of the Wilmington and Weldon Railroad.

Both young men came from wealthy, politically connected families and were descended from Confederate royalty.

According to the August 28 Raleigh Times, 100 or more men assembled at Waynesville with the intention of lynching Strange and Bridgers but were persuaded to disperse. The Asheville Citizen also mentions the incident and says that the deceased's father helped prevent it from getting out of hand.

Strange was granted a change of venue, which shifted his trial from the fall session of the Haywood County superior court to the spring session in Buncombe County. A month before trial, he was moved to the Buncombe County jail. His father, Colonel Strange, came up from Wilmington and paid to have two rooms in the jail that were "neat and comfortable" for his son. He hired servants and a cook. Strange's brother, Robert, stayed with him in jail until the trial, and oh, what a trial it was.

The four-day trial started on Thursday, April 27, 1876, and was held in the chapel of the Asheville Female College, presumably to provide more seating for spectators. Judge Samuel W. Watts of Franklinton, N.C., presided. Josiah Turner, the editor of the Raleigh Sentinel, had given Watts the nickname "Greasy Sam." The judge had a reputation for a disheveled appearance and an impressive ignorance of the law.

Judge Watts casts the longest shadow of all the people involved in the trial. We easily found him mentioned in newspapers as late as 1979, law review articles, and bar association proceedings in 1905, 1928, and 1949. He left his mark or, perhaps more accurately, a dent in North Carolina's legal history.

In July 1876, Watts issued an order for the arrest of Mayor Basil C. Manly and the Raleigh Board of Aldermen. They had been duly elected, but Watts sided with Manly's opponent, John C. Gorman, and ordered them to vacate their offices. When they refused, he held them in contempt. The case went to the N.C. Supreme Court, which quickly sorted the matter out. The Raleigh Sentinel called it "a judicial outrage unparalleled in the history of North Carolina."

In an 1869 case in Warren County northeast of Raleigh, Watts was presiding over the trial of five Black women named Boyd accused of burning a barn. The jury could not agree on a verdict, but Watts was convinced they were guilty, so he devised a novel solution and banished them to South Carolina.

> *"Ordered by the court that an officer of the court escort the defendants to the Southern border of the state, and there leave them."*

The Legal Dream Team of 1876

Thomas Strange was represented by an even dozen defense attorneys. One wonders if they had to push two or even three tables together to seat them all. Most noteworthy among them were Colonel Duncan K. McRae, Colonel B. S. Gaither, and Colonel David Coleman. Interestingly, Major C. M. Stedman was not only part of the defense council but also a character witness for Strange.

As you can imagine, there was a lot of legal back and forth, with each side jockeying for the legal, moral, or evidential high ground. Most of Strange's companions testified, as did townsfolk and even a few people who had encountered the party during their travels from Waynesville toward Cataloochee. Strange had almost as many character witnesses as he did lawyers.

The defense's case boiled down to two assertions: that Thomas Strange's character was so good that it would be pointless to contend that he would lie just to avoid a trip to the gallows and that the jury had to convict him of first-degree murder or acquit him. They had to pick between sentencing Strange to hang or letting him walk free. Manslaughter could not be considered.

*"There could be no manslaughter in this transaction—
the prisoner was either guilty of murder, or he was
innocent; he must be either held accountable for
murder, or he must be sent forth free," said Defense
Attorney Colonel Duncan K. McRae.*

In his written instructions to the jury, Judge Watts concurred that the
only possible verdicts were guilty of first-degree murder or not guilty.
He also included all the names and titles of Strange's character
witnesses. Perhaps the most telling portion of Watts' 1,800-word written
charge to the jury was the following:

*"If you take the circumstances and a part of the
admissions, such as "I killed him," and take the same
circumstances and all his admissions, and you have
two distinct theories or presumptions, one looking to
the guilt and the other to the innocence of the prisoner.
I charge you, the law commands that you shall take the
one looking to innocence; this reason of the maxim
that it is better for ninety and nine guilty persons to
escape than that one innocent man should suffer."*

On Tuesday evening, May 2, after deliberating for a half hour the jury
delivered a verdict of not guilty. Thomas Strange walked out of the court
a free man.

Outrage and Repercussions

A little over a week later, on Thursday night, May 11, concerned citizens
made up of representatives from nearly every county west of the Blue
Ridge held what came to be called the Indignation Meeting. The group
led by General E. R. Hampton adopted eight resolutions, which included
declaring the trial "a farce and mockery of public justice," denouncing
Judge Watts as "one-sided and partial" and describing the ruling that
manslaughter could not be considered "a gross error."

Watts responded to the meeting and coverage of it in the press as follows:

> *"To the Ladies and Gentlemen and Intelligent*
> *Christian People West of the Blue Ridge:*
>
> *The meeting recently held in the College Chapel at*
> *Asheville to denounce me, the jury, and the ladies of*
> *Asheville because Thomas W. Strange was not hanged,*
> *I am sure, does not reflect your sentiments or represent*
> *you. I judge this because that meeting had for its*
> *chairman a man (E. R. Hampton) that has been*
> *publicly denounced in his own country as a horse thief*
> *and was composed chiefly of revenue officials that*
> *have, for the last four or five years played the vampire*
> *upon the poor, unsuspecting people of your*
> *mountains."*

S. W. WATTS, Judge. Asheville, N.C., May 14, 1876

Hampton immediately sued Watts for libel, setting the damages at $25,000. Watts, it appears, did not see this coming.

The trial and acquittal of Thomas Strange would infuriate the citizens of western North Carolina and Haywood County for at least a generation. From the opinion page of the Wednesday, October 26, 1898, North Carolinian newspaper under the heading Thomas W. Strange:

> *"Until this day, the darkest crime that hovers around*
> *the history of the Republican party in the mountains of*
> *North Carolina smirches the record of the court made*
> *by 'Greasy' Sam Watts, who was imported from*
> *Raleigh to save the neck of this wretch from the*
> *expiation of a crime for which he richly deserved a*
> *felon's death at the end of a halter of hemp."*

Thomas Strange went on to become a practicing attorney in 1878 and work for Governor Daniel Gould Fowle in 1888, who would make him a colonel in the state militia. Strange would cherish this title and use it to his dying day. He became a big wheel or at least a well-oiled cog in the state Democratic party. In 1890, he married Florence A. Rogers of Marysville, California. They had two sons: Robert and Thomas.

Strange died of a stroke on August 22, 1899, at the age of 44. His health had been steadily declining for about two years. It's tempting to see karma or the hand of fate in his relatively short life. A life cut short because he cut a life short. However, it seems that while he won the wealth, power, and prestige lottery, he was less fortunate in the health and long life sweepstakes. His father, Colonel Robert Strange, had died of a stroke at the age of 54 in 1877.

Thomas Strange's obituary took up an entire column on the front page of the Wilmington Morning Star. Curiously, it never mentioned the time he shot and killed a man in Haywood County.

5. Defiant Distillers: Stirring Up Trouble

Illicit distillation of liquors. Harper's December 7, 1867. (N.C. Archives: Public Domain).

*"I'm breakin' rocks in the hot sun. I fought the law, and the law won," —
Sonny Curtis, American singer, and songwriter.*

Turn of the century, moonshiners had two natural enemies: informants and revenue agents. Their best defense against both was stealth. They can't arrest you if they can't find you.

Unfortunately, moonshiners not only had to operate their illicit distilleries but also had to get supplies in the form of corn or cornmeal and, depending on the time and place, malted barley, yeast, and sugar. They also needed lots of water, which meant setting up shop near a stream or branch.

Then there are the telltale signs of a still that is up and running. Tracks going in and out of the area. Smoke from the fire. The distinct smell of fermentation. Finally, the shiners had to transport and sell the liquor.

Most moonshiners took the risks in stride. If they got raided, they ran for it or just raised their hands and surrendered. They chalked the raid up to dumb luck. If they had suspicions about which neighbor, competitor, or customer had given them away, it seldom led to more than a fistfight.

The penalty for getting caught making white liquor varied by time and place but was usually one to six months and a fine. Of course, the bigger the operation and the more times you got caught, the greater the penalty.

Moonshiners seeking revenge against informants or shooting it out with lawmen faced greater penalties and significantly higher risks. Resorting to violence could open the door to dying in a hail of lead, decades of imprisonment, or even a trip to the gallows or electric chair.

There are exceptions to this rule: outlaws who solved their problems with bullets or buckshot. Individuals who had a propensity for violence. Some of them were black-hearted killers, while others became legendary figures feared and respected by revenue officers and idolized by their own people.

Lewis Redmond: Moonshine King of the Carolinas

"Major" Lewis Redmond was an outlaw and moonshiner who became a folk hero during Reconstruction for his defiance of federal revenue laws and willingness to fight lawmen. He actively sought out confrontations with revenue agents on more than one occasion. Equal parts hero and villain, he was a product of his time and place.

He acquired the nickname "Major" as a youth while hanging out around Civil War army camps. Born in 1854, he was too young to participate in that conflict.

From Bruce Stewart's book *King of the Moonshiners: Lewis R. Redmond in Fact and Fiction*:

> *"More than any other individual moonshiner in southern Appalachia, Redmond captured the imagination of middle-class Americans during the late nineteenth century. Like Billy the Kid and Jesse James, he became a legendary figure, reflecting people's hopes, needs, and fears."*

While he had been making moonshine and bootlegging for several years, Redmond's outlaw career began on March 1, 1876, when he and his future brother-in-law, Amos Ladd, were confronted by Deputy U.S. Marshals Alfred Duckworth and D. M. Landford in the East Fork area of Transylvania County, NC, near Brevard.

Duckworth had a warrant and was determined to arrest Redmond. In the most common version of the story, Redmond talked Duckworth into holstering his pistol and then shot the deputy in the throat with a derringer handed to him by Ladd.

Authors Bruce Stewart, John Preston Arthur, and Robert A. Cobb all record the shooting that way. Jim Bob Tinsley in *The Land of Waterfalls* mentions a jury of inquest held the day after the shooting that found "The said Alfred F. Duckworth was shot and murdered by one Major Redmon [sic]."

Duckworth died the following day, and Redmond crossed over into South Carolina and began operating out of Pickens County, which at that time was part of a region known as the Dark Corner.

On Thursday night, January 11, 1877, the revenuers set a trap for Redmond and Ladd. Deputy U.S. Marshal Van Hendricks posed as a buyer and set up a meeting at an abandoned house to purchase 25 gallons of moonshine whiskey.

Redmond and Ladd arrived early, kindled a fire in the hearth, took off their boots, and napped while waiting. Around half past midnight, Hendricks and a revenue agent, John Jamison, arrived and engaged them in conversation. At a prearranged time, the rest of the posse, E. H. Barton, W. F. Gary, and Charley White, rushed through the cabin door with drawn guns surrounding the two moonshiners.

From Charleston News and Courier reporter C. McKinley's 1878 article:

> *"Just then, a crowd of men, who had been waiting outside, burst open the door and rushed in on me and surrounded me," Redmond said. "There was a big light in the fireplace, and I saw a dozen guns were cocked and pointed right at me."*

"Several of them jumped upon me at once and held me down and pinioned my arms, and then they turned me over on my back, and Barton and Gary tied my wrists close together."

Redmond alleged that while he was tied, Barton handled him roughly and kicked him. Barton also searched him and took a pocketbook, which Redmond claimed contained $186.

Caught but Not Captured

As they went to leave, Redmond saw an opportunity, and even though his hands were tied, he managed to fight his way through his captors and out the cabin's door into the snow.

He ran around his wagon, jumped over a chestnut log, vaulted a fence, and made it into the woods. He found himself unarmed in the snow in his stocking feet, with no coat or hat.

Any reasonable person would have considered finding shelter to avoid freezing or getting as far away as possible. Redmond was not in the mood to be sensible. He was determined to rescue Amos and get some payback for the rough treatment.

He ran to a nearby house and talked the owner into loaning him a coat, hat, shoes, and a shotgun. He knew the route the revenue officers would have to travel and planned to intercept them.

The revenuers drove right into Redmond's sights when they came down the road with their wagon and the confiscated whiskey wagon.

As the revenue wagon came into range, silhouetted against the snow, Redmond fired. Someone in the wagon returned fire. They abandoned the wagon, took cover, realized they couldn't see Redmond in the darkness, hurriedly remounted the wagon, and drove on.

Redmond had to cease fire for fear of hitting Amos. He pursued on foot, running beside the road. The wagons stopped at the next house, and Amos, who had managed to untie his hands during the melee, slipped away. The posse entered the house. Amos found Redmond, and they faded into the countryside. Barton and Hendricks had been wounded in the exchange of gunfire.

Nine days later, on Saturday morning, January 20, Redmond and at least nine men rode to Barton's house and demanded the return of the $186 and his two mares.

Barton gave Redmond two of his own horses and a check for $100. Barton's wife went with him to cash the check at Easley Station. He sent her home with an escort and with one or both of the horses; accounts vary on this point.

In 1879, Redmond, his wife, and his three children moved back to Swain County, N.C., and settled in a remote cabin beside the Tennessee River near Almond. Revenue agents made a couple of attempts to capture him, but Redmond's location and preparations allowed him to slip away.

On April 7, 1881, his luck ran out. Redmond ran into a concealed party of six revenue officers led by Deputy U.S. Marshal K. S. Ray. They had come in the night before and hid, waiting for him to leave the cabin. According to most reports, he realized his peril, raised his shotgun to shoot, and was caught in a hail of buckshot and rifle bullets from 30 to 50 yards away.

The consensus was that he was hit six times, and some estimate a dozen rounds went through his clothing. He ran and made it somewhere between 150 yards and a half mile before he fell, unable to rise. The officers took Redmond back to the cabin and immediately sent for a doctor. They waited several days before moving him, which likely saved his life.

In July 1881, Billy the Kid (Henry McCarty), also known as William H. Bonney, was shot and killed by Sheriff Pat Garrett. People like to point out that Redmond's capture was on the front page of the New York Times, whereas Billy the Kid's was relegated to page eight.

Redmond's trial took place in August 1881. He pleaded guilty to moonshining and conspiracy for his raids on revenue agents and was sentenced to 10 years at the federal penitentiary in Auburn, N.Y., and fined $2,600. He was never tried for killing Deputy U.S. Marshal Duckworth.

In 1884, South Carolina temperance reformers Sally Taylor and Grace Elmore started advocating for Redmond's pardon and release. On May 16, 1884, President Chester A. Arthur gave Redmond a full and unconditional pardon at the request of U.S. Senator Wade Hampton and Attorney General Benjamin H. Brewster.

Redmond reunited with his family in Pickens County and settled near Walhalla. Dietrich Biemann hired him to run a government distillery there. The whisky was branded as *Redmond's Handmade Corn Whisky* and distributed by F. W. Wagener & Co., Charleston, S.C. The product was enormously popular. Redmond died in Seneca, SC, in 1906 at 51.

Arch Babb: A Family Man with a Winchester

Around daybreak on Tuesday, January 21, 1902, Arch Babb and his partner, Baker Morelock, had a disagreement at an illicit distillery on Shut-In Creek eight miles southwest of Hot Springs, N.C., in Madison County. It quickly escalated into a gunfight. Babb shot Morelock through the chest with a Winchester rifle, and Morelock fired his revolver at Babb, wounding him above or through the right ear.

An article in the January 22 Atlanta Journal said the dispute was over a stolen moonshine still, which Babb suspected Morelock of taking. The article went on to say that the men were brothers-in-law having married sisters. However, our review of census records, marriage records, and family trees showed no familial connection between the men.

Finally, the Journal article predicted that Babb, who had fled the scene under the cover of heavy snow, would likely give himself up because he had a large family and did not want to leave the country. Babb had a wife and seven children.

An Asheville Citizen article published the same day highlighted that both men had come from Greene County, TN. Morelock, recently, while Babb had lived in the Hot Springs area for about a dozen years.

The newspaper's description of that day's weather noted "remarkably low pressure" and a variance of only three degrees in temperature, 33-36°F (1-2 °C) all day. It was cloudy "with a murky heaviness in the air." A drift of sleet set in, which later changed to "a most beautiful snow, some of the flakes being two inches in diameter." Snow fell at intervals. The wind changed from southeast in the morning to northeast and then due north. Exceptional escape weather if one didn't freeze. The consensus was that Babb fled to Tennessee, where he could rely on his family to help him hide.

By Friday, January 24, the local paper, the Madison County Record, published more details from an inquest over the body of Baker Morelock on Shut-In Creek by Squire E N. Fry of Hot Springs. The verdict of the jury was that Baker Morelock came to his death by a gunshot wound to the left breast at the hands of Arch Babb, who shot him with a .44-caliber Winchester rifle. A pistol with one chamber discharged was found near Morelock's body after the shooting.

From the article:

> *"The shooting occurred in a distillery and was brought on, the witness testified, by a disagreement between the deceased and Babb as to some partnership business affairs. After some abusive words exchanged, Babb fired his Winchester rifle at Morelock, who, it is said, fired his pistol about simultaneously."*

The story proved popular, and within a week, it received coverage in seven states. Major newspapers, including Virginia's Norfolk Landmark, Mississippi's Vicksburg Evening Post, Maryland's Baltimore Sun, and Missouri's St. Louis Republic carried the news of a gunfight between two unknown moonshiners on a little-known tributary of the French Broad River.

Eventually, Babb returned to North Carolina. It's not clear if he returned to be with his family or preferred to take his chances with the North Carolina justice system rather than risk an encounter with Morelock's relatives in Tennessee.

His next appearance in newspapers was in the September 22, 1904, Raleigh Morning Post, which noted Solicitor Brown's return to Asheville from Madison County, where he went for Babb's preliminary hearing on the charge of murder in the death of Morelock. Babb was jailed without bail to await the next term of criminal court.

Babb was tried in the February 1905 term of Superior Court in Madison County. Solicitor Brown charged him with second-degree murder. Three witnesses were called: George Ellenberg, W. G. Gregory, and Hester

Babb, Arch's eight-year-old daughter. The jury returned a verdict of not guilty. Babb died in 1924 in Hendersonville, N.C., at 67.

Garrett Hedden's Red Record

In 1900, Garrett Hedden cast a long shadow over the mountains of Polk County, TN. He was a renowned moonshiner and outlaw known for his uncanny accuracy with a Winchester. He was said to have killed four men, a total that would grow over time.

In 1898, he had shot and killed his own brother, who was engaged in a drunken brawl. Local newspapers complained that "no one had sufficient nerve to cause his arrest." He traveled the countryside and walked the streets of nearby towns unmolested with his rifle in hand.

In August 1900, the stage was set for a shootout between Hedden and a raiding party of seven lawmen and citizens. J. B. Altom, chief raiding deputy of the Knoxville Internal Revenue office, had received definite information about an illegal distillery in the Hedden settlement near Frog Mountain. He traveled to Cleveland, TN, and gathered a posse for the raid.

They left Cleveland at dark and spent all night traveling 35 miles (56 km), arriving at the banks of the Ocoee River at 6:00 a.m. the following day. They left their driver and teams there and proceeded "thence afoot over a rough, mountainous country until 9:00 am."

They had a guide to take them to Riley Hedden's house, and the moonshine still he was operating in a hollow 200 yards from his backdoor. While the moonshiners went about their routine, gathering and chopping firewood and tending the still, the raiding party quietly closed in and surrounded them.

Riley and another man were arrested at the house. Riley's nephew, Gus, and two others were arrested at the still. According to the Knoxville Journal and Tribune, the raiding party found a 65-gallon (246 L) copper still with 3,000 gallons (11,360 L) of beer, as well as a good quantity of meal, mash, and whiskey, were destroyed.

The raiders handcuffed the men and gathered them at the house; everything was going according to plan until Garrett Hedden rode over the hill on a mule carrying his Winchester across the saddle.

The following account is from a 1902 article in *The Atlantic* by Leonidas Hubbard, Jr.:

> *"Then, the revenues jumped into the house and behind the corncrib and began to shoot at Garret," said Gus Hedden. "They shot seven or eight shots before he moved. Then he slid off his mule and laid down behind a log."*

Constable C. B. Cash was restraining Garrett's brother, Riley. He pulled Cash out into the open several times, either in the hopes that Cash would release him rather than risk being shot by Garrett or hoping to escape after Garrett hit Cash. Altom leveled his gun at Riley, who abandoned his attempts to drag Cash into the path of one of Garrett's bullets.

> *"The revenues threatened to kill us if we didn't go out and get Garret to go away," Gus continued. "We told 'em we couldn't do nothing with Garret. So we all laid* X *there behind the house, and Garret laid behind his log with his Winchester, scaring the revenues powerful nigh into fits. When it got too dark to see, they took us and sneaked out."*

The August 21, Nashville Tennessean described the shootout as follows:

> *"On a signal from one of the prisoners, the horseman, who proved to be Garrett (Hedden), sprang from his horse and threw himself in a clump of underbrush. He opened fire on Deputy Pierce, who responded with a*

double-barreled shotgun. Other members of the posse took up the shooting, and for a moment, there was a fusillade. No one was hit, and (Hedden) effected his escape. The other five men were carried back to Knoxville."

The party and its five prisoners traveled back to the wagons and teams beside the river and arrived back in Cleveland shortly before midnight Wednesday. The skirmish further established Garrett's reputation as a man to be feared. Ironically, his deadly reputation would have fatal consequences.

"Bring a Coffin"

On Friday night, January 3, 1908, Polk County Sheriff Burch E. Biggs and his deputies boarded the L&N train at Benton. They headed to Etowah to meet Sheriff Pryor Watson of Monroe County and his deputies.

The mission of this six-man posse was to finally apprehend Garrett Hedden for the now decade-old murder of his brother, Bill, and to find and destroy the illegal distillery he had been operating on Lost Creek about three miles north of Reliance for several years. Sheriff Biggs was determined to arrest Hedden before his term in office expired.

An article published in the January 9 edition of the Knoxville Sentinel asserted that Garrett had explicitly warned the sheriff against attempting to effect his arrest.

> *"According to report, Hedden had more than once sent word to Sheriff Biggs of Polk County that if the officer should ever come after him, 'he better bring along a coffin.'"*

That Saturday morning, rain saturated the leaves and underbrush around Lost Creek. The steady downpour allowed the raiding party to quietly close in on the moonshine operation. Once more, the posse had a guide to direct them to their objective.

A 1924 article in the Nashville Banner said the posse managed to crawl through the underbrush within 20 yards of the "illicit distillery, which was well-fortified" and surround it.

Garrett was seen exiting the still house, and when he had gotten about 10 yards from it, Biggs commanded him to halt and throw up his hands. Instead, the moonshiner whirled and darted for the still house. The officers were not about to risk Garrett getting his hands on his Winchester; they opened fire.

From the Chattanooga Daily Times:

> *"Just as he entered the door, the sheriff gave the command to fire, and the whole posse fired, the volley of buckshot completely riddling the mountaineer's body from head to heel. When later picked up, his whole back was found to be perforated with buckshot."*

And so, the life and exploits of the formidable and feared moonshiner Garrett Hedden came to a close. He was 52 years old.

(Editor's note: Hedden was spelled multiple ways in news reports and documents, including Henden, Hadden, Headen, and Heddon.)

Banty Gregory's Reign of Terror

In December 1921, Josiah "Joe Banty" Gregory launched a revenge campaign against the Oliver and Sparks families in Cades Cove, TN. Gregory got the nickname "Banty" because of his short stature and aggressive manner, like a bantam rooster. He and two of his sons had been convicted of making moonshine whiskey multiple times. Joe had a reputation for producing a high-quality corn whiskey that was in great demand.

The trouble began on December 8, when Deputy Sheriff John A. Myers and Constable George Brown raided Gregory's still. Although it was later revealed that a surveyor tipped off the sheriff, Banty blamed the Olivers. Unintentionally, the officers made matters worse when they borrowed a team of mules and a wagon from William Oliver to haul away the large copper still and confiscated whiskey.

William Oliver and his son, John Oliver, were Primitive Baptist preachers. Both were outspoken opponents of liquor consumption in general and moonshining in particular. John was also the local mail carrier.

The night after the raid, John Oliver looked out his window and discovered his barn was on fire. John, his wife, Nancy, and their children sprang into action to save the five horses trapped inside.

Oliver was able to get three of the horses out fairly quickly. The stalls of the farm's draft horses, Joe and Gib, were surrounded by flames in the center of the barn. Joe was too frightened to leave his stall. John took off his undershirt and placed it over the horse's head; this allowed him to lead the horse to safety. The barn was becoming an inferno, and his repeated attempts to get Gib out failed. The horse perished in the flames.

From *Cades Cove: The Life and Death of a Southern Appalachian Community 1818-1937*, by Durwood Dunn:

> *"In the meantime, many neighbors had come over and began trying to save the crib, which stood close to the barn. This crib contained a year's harvest of corn and all the farm machinery. (11-year-old) Lucille and (14-year-old) Wayne carried dozens of tubs of water from the branch as the neighbors placed wet tow sacks on the crib roof, putting out the flames and wetting it down."*

As the family took stock of what had been lost and what had been salvaged, word came that William Oliver's barn had also been set on fire and was a total loss, including mules, a wagon, farm equipment, hay, and some cattle.

"The fire destroyed about twenty-five years of our hard labor," William Howell Oliver later recalled, according to Dunn.

John Oliver slept with a rifle in his only remaining barn for months after the fire, just in case. The cold and somber winter of 1921–22 had more startling surprises for the residents of Cades Cove.

A Disastrous Prank

On Christmas Eve, Joe Banty's son Earl and his friend, Perry Tipton, played a prank on John and Francis "France" Sparks. The two young men caught the Sparks boys walking home in the dark, jumped out, impersonated Deputy Myers and Constable Brown, and pretended to arrest them.

The victims knew something wasn't right. It was clear to them that the two men confronting them were too short to be the lawmen. The Sparks brothers decided to fight it out with the two impostors. Earl was struck in the head and face several times with a flashlight. Once the fight was over and the boys were identified, John Sparks took them into the house, where his mother bandaged Earl's wounds.

Earl's injuries enraged the Gregory family. There was only one way to remove this stain on their honor: swift retaliation. Joe Banty and his son, Dana, caught up with the Sparks boys the next day at the Sparks family Christmas celebration at the home of Fonze Cable. Joe Banty and Dana invited themselves in and were welcomed. What happened next was as unexpected as it was violent.

From *Cades Cove: A Personal History* by Judge William Wayne Oliver (John Oliver's son):

"After an hour or so, Joe remarked they should be getting home. At that, Dana picked up a wood fire poker and knocked John Sparks out of his chair and into the fireplace. Dana and Joe then pulled their revolvers and began shooting, wounding Asa and John Sparks. Calmly reloading their guns, they backed out of the house, mounted their horses, rode away, and disappeared from home."

(Editor's Note: Newspaper articles place the shooting at the home of John Marr. Dunn, in his book, says the incident occurred at the Dan Myers home.)

A December 27 Knoxville Journal and Tribune article reported that John and Asa were in Knoxville General Hospital. John suffered three intestinal wounds, and two perforations were found in his stomach. He was not expected to live. Asa, the paper identified him as A.C. Sparks, was shot in the back. He was expected to recover, but the next day, his condition worsened. It's not clear if the Gregorys mistook Asa for his cousin, France, or if he was just shot in the confusion. Eventually, both men recovered.

On Sunday, New Year's Day, 1922, Tom Sparks rode up and asked John Oliver to come to a meeting at Deputy Myers' house. Gathered around a bonfire there, in the presence of Constable Brown and two Justices of the Peace, Tom ordered his grandson, Wade Sparks, to tell the assembled men what he knew about the burning of the Oliver barns. Wade Sparks confessed that Joe Banty and his wife, Elvira, paid him and Dana Gregory $50 each to burn the barns. He subsequently testified to this in court.

About a week later, Joe Banty and Dana Gregory were found hiding in the attic of a relative's house and arrested.

On July 5, 1922, Joe and Dana Gregory were found guilty of two counts of felonious assault and of assault with intent to commit murder in the second degree. They were sentenced to three to 21 years for the former and 15 years for the latter. They appealed to the Tennessee Supreme Court, which affirmed their conviction on October 7, 1923.

On October 19, 1922, Dana was convicted of setting fire to John Oliver's barn, and Joe and Elvira were found guilty as accessories. They were sentenced to from two to 21 years in the state penitentiary. A week later, Judge Sam Brown overturned the conviction because it was based entirely on Wade Sparks' testimony, who was an admitted accomplice to the crime.

On December 24, 1923, The Gregorys were pardoned by Tennessee Governor Austin Peay as part of a Christmas pardon list. It seems that justice came up a bit short, given the nature of their crimes.

According to Dunn, when Joe Gregory died in 1933, at 62, John Oliver was asked to conduct his funeral. He agreed to perform this service. Oliver practiced a faith and dedication seldom seen in any time or place.

Ike Strong and His Moonshine Citadel

Shortly before sunrise on March 28, 1923, a 22-man posse led by Prohibition Agent William B. Saylor and Deputy U.S. Marshal Adrian Metcalf quietly surrounded the home of Isaac "Ike" Strong on Beech Fork, near Asher, KY, about 25 miles (40 km) north of Harlan.

Ike, his wife Della, and his brother George had some surprises in store for the officers. At about 5:00 am, as the men were moving into position and Agent Saylor started toward the front door to serve the warrant, the situation went sideways.

Someone in the house spotted Deputy Sheriff Kelly Walker and fired through a window, hitting him in the chest. He wheeled and ran for cover but was struck in the head by a second shot and died instantly.

The posse opened fire, and chaos erupted. All three of the Strongs were seen firing through the cabin windows. Metcalf had taken cover behind a pile of cordwood about 20 feet from the front door, and bullets perforated the wood, some going entirely through the stack of the thick wood, but none of the rounds found him.

The Owensboro Messenger-Inquirer carried the following description of the firefight:

> *"Companions of the slain officer concentrated a withering fire from high-powered rifles on the house from vantage points behind trees and ledges. As the steel-jacketed slugs were sent ripping through the walls of the building, the fire of the defenders became desultory and finally ceased."*

When the firing from the house stopped, officers entered the cabin and found all three of the Strongs: Ike, age 47, Della, age 44, and George, age 21, sprawled on the cabin floor dead. Multiple articles reported that Della had a repeating rifle clutched in her hands.

The posse was shocked to discover the couple's five children huddled in a corner under a bed, miraculously uninjured. Officers were at a loss to explain the children's survival, as the house was riddled with bullets.

An article in the Middlesboro Daily News says about 75 shots were fired, and the battle lasted about two and a half minutes. The Frankfort State Journal quoted a state prohibition report that said several hundred shots were fired.

Searching behind the house, the agents found three stills and another surprise: the Strongs had built fortifications. They discovered one moonshine still near the house and two stills in a still house over a spring about 250 yards away, along with 700 gallons (2,650 L) of beer. Just in front of the still house was a smaller log building with small portholes or firing slits.

They discovered another heavily constructed cabin with portholes, a bed, and a stove 150 yards further up the hillside. This house overlooked all approaches to the stills and was thought to have been an observation post. It reminded one observer of blockhouses used by the Spaniards in Cuba during the Spanish-American war.

The prohibition report stated that it was fortunate the officers did not catch the moonshiners working at the still, for they would have been in a position to hold off 100 men, and their actions demonstrated they had no intention of surrendering.

Epilogue

Lewis Redmond escaped arrest, pursued revenue agents, and retired to a mountain hideout. But the revenue agents came for him, and he was shot, imprisoned, and eventually pardoned. He became the most popular man in South Carolina and, ultimately, a legend.

Arch Babb fled but, after two years on the run, decided to take his chances in the North Carolina courts. He was quick, lucky in that he wasn't standing three inches farther to the right during his gunfight with Morelock, and able to convince a jury that he acted in self-defense.

Garrett Hedden moved about with impunity due to his deadly reputation, which, in time, caused him to die in a hail of buckshot. In that same raid, his son was wounded, and his nephew also died.

Banty Gregory dodged an arson conviction and was convicted of two counts of felonious assault in July 1922 but made it home for Christmas 1923 due to a questionable pardon. He didn't need luck; he had political connections.

Ike Strong, his wife, and his brother shot it out, surrounded and outnumbered seven to one. They might have survived the battle if they could have made it to their hillside fort, but it's not clear if the five children would have.

6. The 33-Year Fugitive

Portable Sawmill Cutting Government Logs (NARA: Public Domain).

"Every shot that kills ricochets." — Gilbert Parker, Canadian novelist, and British politician, from A Romany of the Snows.

On Friday, October 26, 1933, George W. Franklin, a prosperous cattle rancher from southwest Louisiana, walked into the office of Madison County Sheriff Guy English in Marshall, N.C., and announced that his name was James Lunsford. He was there to turn himself in for the fatal shooting of his cousin, Eli "Bud" Lunsford, in 1900. Franklin appeared back in his native mountains and surrendered to be tried for a murder charge, in the words of an Associated Press reporter, "apparently out of a clear sky."

The Associated Press (AP), a news agency that has provided content to newspapers and other media since 1846, picked up the story. The AP is sometimes referred to as a wire service because its original news transmissions were by telegraph.

This propelled the story beyond Lunsford's native North Carolina and his adopted state of Louisiana, which knew him as Franklin. Newspapers far and wide ran the story from Montreal, Quebec's Gazette, to Texas' Brownsville Herald. The Los Angeles Times carried a photo of Franklin looking dapper wearing a large cowboy hat. While the story didn't make it into the New York Times, it made the New York Age, Brooklyn Times Union, and Buffalo Evening News.

While most of these reports described the 58-year-old Lunsford as "Bronzed and looking years younger than his age," the Charlotte Observer described his appearance as "Gray and worn by the years." It's hard not to see this as anything other than crime-never-pays editorializing from the paper.

Describing the story as "An Oddity in the News," the Shreveport, LA, Times lauded him for his courage, noting, "This makes news, as does any other happening in which some citizen suddenly displays honesty in an extraordinary manner."

The question everyone wanted answered was why he had come back. What motivated him to risk being tried for first-degree murder? For all intents and purposes, this was a forgotten crime. After all, he appeared to have made a clean getaway. He had money, a family, respect in the community where he now lived, and a large ranch.

Why would he take the risk? Not only could he spend the rest of his life in prison, but the death penalty was also a possibility. North Carolina had an electric chair and executed five people in 1933, 20 in 1934, and 11 in 1935.

Most of the newspaper reports had the same short and cryptic response from Lunsford.

> *"I know I was justified," he said. "I just wanted to get this thing cleared up and off my mind." Articles covering his surrender and trial carried this one explanation, which he declined to expand upon.*

Reporters were no more successful in getting comments from Violet, his wife, who accompanied him from Louisiana. A report in the Asheville Citizen mentions they were both glad to be back in the mountains and that she had no desire to return to her former home in the Big Pine community.

What motivated Lunsford to return and stand trial? Did the ever-present possibility of a stranger placing a hand on his shoulder and saying, "James Lunsford, you are under arrest for the murder of Bud Lunsford," wear him down? Was it a need for validation? Did he need a judge and jury to agree that he acted in self-defense? Was it a simple need for closure? If found guilty or not guilty, it would finally be over. Or was it guilt over having ended Bud Lunsford's life?

We have one clue from the October 28, 1933, Asheville Times. It appears that Franklin or his wife forgot one of the cardinal rules of fugitive life: Sever all communications.

From the article:

> *"Madison County relatives are reported to have known of his whereabouts for several years. About three months ago, J. Hubert Davis, clerk of Madison County Superior Court, received a letter from one of the relatives disclosing that Lunsford might be found in Dequiney, LA, under the name of Franklin. Davis turned the letter over to W. Howard Norriss, of Marshall, a nephew of James Lunsford."*

A Deadly Encounter

The incident occurred on Wednesday, August 29, 1900, when James Lunsford returned from a work trip to his home in the Big Pine community and found his cousin, Bud, drunk and attempting to enter his house. James contends that Bud had been paying "unwelcome attention" to his wife, Violet. In another version of the story, the cousins were in a dispute over a recent school board election. It is entirely possible that both were true, and that trouble had been brewing between them for some time.

Words were exchanged, and Bud left. James armed himself with a pistol (a .44 caliber revolver, according to one published report) and went in pursuit. He had a fairly good idea his cousin was headed to John Randall's sawmill on Anderson Branch, a little over a mile away, where it was alleged one could buy moonshine liquor.

James confronted Bud about the attempted break-in, and things quickly escalated from words to violence to deadly force. According to a report in the October 28, 1933, Asheville Citizen, witnesses said Bud drew a knife and advanced on his cousin. James drew the revolver and shot the ground in front of Bud, who, despite the warning, continued his advance. James is said to have fired twice, fatally wounding Bud, who died nine days later. James Lunsford disappeared from Madison County immediately after the shooting.

The Sunday, September 2, 1900, Raleigh Morning Post gave this report:

> *"There was a fight last Wednesday on Anderson Branch, seven miles west of Marshall, between James Lunsford and Bud Lunsford, in which Bud was shot through the body. His physicians say there is no chance for his recovery. The man that used the pistol is in the woods with officers close on him. The affair is very much regretted."*

The article went on to point out that:

> *"Madison County is needing a special term of court, a good rain, and a compulsory system of education."*

It is believed that friends helped Lunsford make his way to Flag Pond, TN, just across the state line. John Randall, the sawmill owner, was tried as an accomplice after the fact and served four months "on the roads" for aiding in Lunsford's escape.

There is a saying that is well traveled and well known in law enforcement, military, and even martial arts circles: it's better to be tried by 12 than carried by six. The 12, of course, refers to jurors, and the 6 refers to pallbearers. The point is that if you use deadly force, you better be able to justify it in a court of law, but you have to survive the encounter first.

Having said that, there are always a few who choose a third option: shoot first and flee. There are many problems with choosing what is behind the metaphorical door number three. Two stand out. First, there is a better than even chance that they will catch you, and many, if not most people, will see fleeing as an admission of guilt. Second, you can never go home again. At least not without risking losing your freedom and possibly your life. Lunsford chose to flee.

Knowing he couldn't stay hidden just across the state line, he waited long enough for Violet to slip away and join him there. They moved on to West Virginia. Adopting the name George W. Franklin, Lunsford found employment in the coalfields and mines there.

Coal mining in 1900 was a dangerous occupation, and it is still today. Out of 485,544 coal miners working in 1901, there were 1,574 work-related deaths. The numbers almost doubled over the next 10 years. Using the assumed name and keeping a low profile, he was able to put some money away. Not easy to do on a coal miner's salary. Miners averaged a 12-hour workday and were paid $1.70 per day, or $10.20 a week.

On September 30, 1901, Lunsford's situation worsened. N.C. Governor Charles B. Aycock offered a reward of $200 (about $6,800 today) for his apprehension and delivery to the sheriff of Madison County. Lunsford was now an outlaw with a price on his head. Later newspaper reports mention a standing reward of $300.

At some point, the couple moved south to Louisiana, where they continued to travel under the radar and use the name Franklin. The 1910 census found George and Violet Franklin living in Calcasieu, LA. The entry also notes that they were both born in North Carolina. The 1930 census shows the couple in Dequincy, LA, and mentions an adopted daughter, Mary, who was 14. Over time, Franklin established himself as a prosperous rancher and farmer. He became a minister as well. He appeared to have succeeded in leaving his past behind.

A Trio of Reluctant Witnesses

The sheriff was unsure how to handle a 33-year-old murder case and contacted N.C. Solicitor Zeb V. Nettles in Asheville, 21 miles to the southeast. Franklin was released on a $1,500 cash bond, which was not an issue for the Louisiana cattle baron. His trial for first-degree murder was set for the November 1933 term of Madison County Superior Court.

The case was almost immediately continued until the February 1934 term of court. Putting together a murder case is very time-consuming and intensive. A capital case where a defendant's life is on the line was not taken lightly, even in 1933. A homicide case that occurred more than three decades ago added to the difficulty of trial preparation. Franklin was allowed to return home to Louisiana, a journey of almost 900 miles by train. The cash bond and his word acted as a guarantee that he would return to face trial.

The court found three living eyewitnesses: John Randall, the sawmill owner; James Roberts, who was present that night; and Matilda Cousins, who lived next door to the sawmill and witnessed the incident from her yard. All three were reluctant to testify.

John Randall was in Central Prison in Raleigh, serving a 17-year sentence for killing George Plemmons, his next-door neighbor, in Barnard, the previous Christmas Eve. Randall's wife had run next door to seek protection from him. When Plemmons refused to let Randall enter his home to retrieve her, Randall shot him with a 12-gauge shotgun, killing him instantly.

The incident was not the first time Randall went to jail for murder. In 1908, he received a 30-year sentence for clubbing his first wife to death. In 1900, she was alleged to have smuggled escape tools to him when he was held in the Marshall jail for being an accessory after the fact in James Lunsford's escape. Newspaper reports do not give either woman's name, referring to each of them only as Mrs. John Randall.

On August 29, 1934, the State of North Carolina vs. James Lunsford alias George Franklin was once again continued for a year. Representatives for the prosecution and defense had traveled to Lockhart, S.C., in a taxi to bring Matilda Cousins, described as a "star witness," back to the court to testify. Cousins had refused to return to Madison County with them. Nettles made plans to have Cousins back in August 1935 to testify at the hearing under arrest if necessary. This plan never came to fruition.

An article in the August 25, 1935, Greensboro Daily News summed up the situation this way: "… but one witness is in the penitentiary, one has refused to return for the trial, and the third remains silent at his home in the Big Pine section."

On August 29, 1935, a full 35 years after the shooting and 22 months after Franklin voluntarily surrendered to stand trial for the killing, Prosecutor Nettles presented a nol. Pros. Plea – a prosecutor's formal notice of abandonment of the action against the defendant. The inability to get two of the three remaining witnesses to testify rendered the case untenable. Franklin was a free man. He, his wife, Violet, and his daughter, Mary, returned to their ranch in Louisiana.

As is so often true when examining events long past, there are more facts left unknown than known, and you never truly know what the motivations of the moment were; perhaps even the principals involved aren't always certain.

We will never know what was on James Lunsford's mind when he armed himself and pursued his cousin. Was he thinking, "I'm going to set Bud straight once and for all," or was his notion more like, "I'm going to kill that son of a gun?" And in that fatal moment of conflict and confusion at the sawmill, did he fire into the ground to warn his cousin to stop advancing with the knife, or did he simply miss with his first shot?

Here's what we do know. James Lunsford killed Bud Lunsford. He fled to avoid trial. Changed his name. Became a miner, a rancher, and finally a minister, then despite having become prominent, wealthy, and respected, he risked everything to answer for the crime. And Violet shared his journey every step of the way.

George Franklin died on March 17, 1961, at the age of 85. Violet died about a month later, on April 27, 1961. She was 82. Their obituaries mention their adopted daughter, Mary Keys, four grandchildren, and three great-grandchildren. There is no mention of their birth names or references to their lives outside Louisiana.

7. A Life in Liquor and Blood

Confiscated whiskey between 1921 and 1932. (LOC: Public Domain).

"When two men fight over a woman, it's the fight they want, not the woman." — *Brendan Behan, Irish poet, short story writer, novelist, playwright, and Irish Republican activist.*

It's a situation we've all seen a thousand times in movies and on TV: two armed men face off in a dusty street in the 1870s in the southwestern United States, determined to settle things once and for all. Their dispute may be over a gambling debt, a stolen deed, or the reputation of being the fastest gun in the West.

Only this time, it wasn't a couple of cowboys with six guns but two Black men in a predominately Black work camp run by the Lumber Mineral Co. in Hot Springs, N.C., in 1904. And the dispute was over a young woman named Mary, who worked at the company store.

Men have been fighting over women since the beginning of time. As a law enforcement officer, I have often responded to such scenes. Put a pin in that; we'll talk more about it at the end of the chapter.

Like most camps set up by lumber and mining companies, it provided meals, some medical attention, mostly by barbers, and a commissary or company store to provide other goods.

Fred Avery and Joe Bryant both showed interest in Mary. It's not known if she had feelings for either of the men or if she enjoyed their attention. The men's rivalry ended Saturday night at nine o'clock on January 16, in front of the commissary.

A crowd had gathered to see the fight. We don't have much in the way of details regarding the shootout. Witnesses said both men were armed: Avery with a Winchester Model 94 lever-action rifle chambered in .32 Winchester Special, and Bryant with a handgun and large knife. The Nashville Graphic tells us that there were two shots fired, both from Avery's rifle. One amputated Bryant's left thumb, and the other hit him almost center mass, going all the way through his body and killing him.

A later report in the Raleigh Morning Post said Avery "was sentenced for seven years for the killing of a desperate (man) who was at the time loading a pistol for the supposed purpose of killing Avery."

The Madison County Record, Marshall, N.C., stated: "The trouble originated over a woman and was augmented by the free use of Prohibition whisky now on tap at Hot Springs."

Liquor and violence were themes that would run through and shape Avery's life.

Multiple newspaper stories say Avery was immediately taken to the Marshall jail to avoid further trouble. The Raleigh News and Observer noted, "After the shooting, Avery was arrested and taken to Marshall jail for fear that the [Blacks] would attempt to lynch him. It was said at the time that the feeling against Avery was intense and that had he not been removed, he would never have been tried by a court."

While it is possible that Bryant was popular and well-liked and Avery was not, it seems more likely that the lumber company's workforce was "greatly excited" because they didn't feel the shooting was a fair fight.

The state convened a grand jury in Marshall. After hearing evidence and statements, it found probable cause to send the killing to Superior Court. The same grand jury also returned a true bill against the Southern Railway Co. and the Southern Express Co. for violating the law by delivering liquor packages in Madison County.

Judge B. F. Long of Statesville presided over the criminal term of the Madison County court with nine murder cases on the docket. A February 1904 article in the Raleigh Morning Post characterized Long as "severe on evildoers." In that same piece, the paper quotes the judge directly.

> *"I have had the misfortune usually in this beautiful mountain country to find large criminal dockets,"* Long said. *"I am told that in this border country from Alleghany to Haywood (eight counties), more men have been killed since the war than lost their lives in the Spanish-American war. It is appalling."*

A U.S. Department of Veterans Affairs factsheet puts U.S. Spanish-American War battle deaths at 385 (including the 268 sailors on the USS Maine) and 2,061 additional deaths, mostly from yellow fever. The war lasted from April to August 1898. Long was speaking in February 1904, five years after the war.

The State vs. Fred Avery was first on the docket and tried. After hearing the evidence, the jury found Avery guilty of manslaughter. He was given a seven-year sentence.

During that term of court, Peter Smith was also convicted of the capital crime of first-degree rape. Condemned to hang, he was the last man North Carolina executed by hanging in Madison County—more on Smith in another chapter.

Governor Robert B. Glenn declined to pardon Avery or Smith in September 1905. Glenn was in hot water for the recent commutation of William Exum's sentence from hanging to life in prison at hard labor for the shooting death of his stepson, Guy Walston, near Kinston in Lenoir County.

Exum was a wealthy and well-connected man who had shot his unarmed stepson twice after he had made a disparaging remark about Exum. Exum's wife managed to get between them in an effort to save her son, but Exum reached around her to deliver the fatal shot to Walston's head. After killing Walston, he fled the scene and later resisted arrest.

From a September 1905 Raleigh Morning Post article about the governor's refusal to grant Avery a pardon:

> "Neither trial judge nor solicitor recommend a pardon; no evidence was sent up to disclose the nature of the crime; only a short petition was filed, which throws no light on the case. Finding nothing in the case to warrant me granting the petition, the pardon is refused."

Then, in September 1906, Glenn did a complete about-face and pardoned Avery. This time, the proclamation stated:

> "Defendant has already been confined over two years. The evidence convinces me that the man acted in self-defense and should not have been convicted. He was guarding a house and was set upon by deceased. The trial judge, solicitor, and county officers recommend a pardon. The defendant was a man of good character.

The pardon is granted, conditioned on his good behavior. "

What a difference a year made. The pardon statement in no way matches the newspaper reports from the time of the shooting or the evidence and testimony that convicted Avery for it. Oddly, none of the newspaper reports about the pardon mention this complete and total incompatibility, nor do they mention the apparent change of heart of the judge and solicitor.

A Shooting on Depot Street

In June 1912, Fred Avery made the headlines again, this time for shooting Will Maxwell in Asheville. Like the Hot Springs shooting, there was a woman involved or at least present. Viola Nesbit, a Black woman, was walking with Avery in the alley just a few feet off Depot Street on the banks of Town Branch around 9 p.m. on a Friday.

According to her account, Maxwell, also Black, approached them and asked Avery what he was doing out so late. Maxwell was drinking at the time, and after a few words passed between the men, he threw the bottle at Avery, striking him in the head. She also said that Maxwell threw rocks at Avery, who walked off about five steps, drew a revolver from his pocket, and fired three times, hitting Maxwell twice. Maxwell ran about 10 feet to the rear of one of the buildings, where he fell on his face and died. Avery immediately "took to his heels" and was not captured despite an intensive search.

Other witnesses declared that the two men did not speak to each other at all and that Avery shot Maxwell as he walked past the couple. According to the June 1 Asheville Citizen, Depot Street was "well filled with pedestrians at the time the fatal affair took place."

Coroner E. R. Morris was notified of the shooting and immediately responded to the scene. The body was removed to a funeral home for examination. One bullet went into Maxwell's back and passed through the left cavity of his heart. This was the fatal wound. The other bullet entered his back about four inches from the first, entering his shoulder.

We have no way of knowing if Maxwell knew Avery or Nesbit prior to the incident. We do know that Avery and Maxwell both worked for Southern Railway. Maxwell was a porter. The article didn't specify Avery's position with the railroad. It went on to state that he was living in Knoxville and vacationing in Asheville at the time of the shooting. Avery never stood trial for this crime.

Showdown in Danville

Avery's next appearance in the news in January 1934 in Danville, VA, was his last. Louis Fuller struck him in the head with an iron bar during a fight. He died from a skull fracture 12 days later at Providence Hospital.

An article in the Danville, VA, Bee about the fight called it "a quarrel between neighbors," but an earlier report said it resulted from "a bootleg war." Fuller hit Avery on the head with an iron bar, and Harry Penn shot Fuller in both legs with a shotgun. Fuller claimed that Avery had brought the iron bar with him and attempted to strike him with it and that he took the bar away from Avery and used it to hit Avery on the side of the head and about the body with it. After Avery was down, Penn shot Fuller, according to witnesses.

An autopsy showed that Avery had a fracture of the skull in the frontal area and that brain tissue in the area had been sufficiently injured by concussion to cause his death.

At the time of the melee, Fuller was out on bond to arrange his affairs before serving 90 days on the city farm for violating liquor laws. Avery and Penn had also been brought up on liquor charges but were set free. There was some speculation that the men had quarreled over testimony at that term of court.

A woman named Ethel Smith was also said to have been involved in the fight, and Fuller was also charged with assaulting her. Two months later, Fuller was sentenced to 10 years in prison for killing Avery.

The significant events of Fred Avery's life appear to have involved liquor and violence. From his late teens working at the lumber camp in Hot Springs to his death in what was likely his mid-50s in Danville, he seemed to go from one scrape to another. Perhaps the portions of his life that weren't recorded in the newspapers and court records held some human connections and genuine accomplishments. All we know for certain is that he gunned down two men and died in a brawl about liquor violations.

Three's a Brawl: Asheville 1990s

With all deference to writer Brendan Behan, whose quote opened this chapter, sometimes when men fight over a woman, it is the woman they want, and sometimes that changes in the course of the fight or after it. Let me share a less deadly and less tragic episode about men fighting over a woman from my time as a police officer in Asheville.

The city changes at 8:00 p.m. on a Friday. It's almost like flipping a switch. At this temporal tipping point, the type of tourist you encounter changes. The interest in loud music, alcohol, and pub food ramps up appreciably, as do calls for officers to handle the occasional disturbance. Police working downtown will respond to a front or a side door and encounter troublemakers at that point. The suspects are searched, cuffed, and transported to jail. They are usually on their way downtown before the dispatched backup officers arrive.

Before cell phones, the bar staff or club manager called in problems, usually just once. It's different today; if someone is not recording the action on their phone, they're on the line with 911, giving a blow-by-blow description of the incident in real time.

On an early fall evening, I was dispatched to an argument between two men at a nightclub adjacent to a hotel. Like most Friday night calls, I had little in the way of information about what I was heading into. When I arrived on the scene, I discovered the bar emptied into the parking lot and a crowd surrounding two men squared off against each other. Both combatants showed signs of the fight, including torn clothes and bloody faces.

I advised my dispatcher that I had arrived and described the situation. I could hear police sirens being activated in the distance as backup headed my way to help and, in some cases, to see what was going on. Assured assistance was on its way. I asked a bystander about the fight and if anyone had seen a weapon on either subject.

The skinny red-haired man responded negatively to the possibility of the weapons and stated the "argument" was over a young woman. At that point, I noticed a tall blonde woman who appeared to be in her early 20s attempting to break up the fight by yelling and pulling on the two men.

During a lull in the fisticuffs, she managed to get the attention of the older-looking pugilist and shouted something that caused the blood to drain from his face. With a new look of fear, he quickly abandoned the fight, running straight at me, sidestepping, and disappearing into the crowd just before he reached me.

The second combatant took off in pursuit of the first. I was determined not to let the second fighter escape, having lost the first. As the big man ran in my direction, chasing his rival, I grabbed him, intending to use his momentum to take him to the ground. The move was good in theory, but I came up short on application.

In an instant of whirling motion, I found myself behind the man, dragged like a dislodged bull rider. My glasses flew off in an unknown direction. The two-legged bull pulled me across the parking lot. Despite his determined efforts to dislodge me, I found myself on his back. I was not sure in the flailing about how I ended up there. Another officer arrived;

he said I looked like a kid attempting to ride a goat at a rodeo, refusing to let go.

I finally overpowered the Brahma bull or billy goat (depending on your perspective) with the assistance of several officers. He was handcuffed, transported to jail, charged with many appropriate offenses, and had his bail set. After the paperwork was done and a few hours of cooldown time had elapsed, I returned to jail to speak to the man, get a statement, and ask what in the wide, wide world of sports had caused this fracas.

I had learned that public fights generally have a reason. It might not make sense to the spectator because logic is usually replaced by rage.

It turned out that the young blond woman was engaged to my arrestee. Earlier that evening, he had been working his shift at a convenience store in West Asheville when he received a call from a friend at the bar, who had seen her there with an ex-boyfriend who had moved out of state the previous year. The friend had also noticed that the couple had walked to the bar from the hotel next door.

On hearing this report, my now-jailed acquaintance bolted from the store. In his haste and distress, he left the store unlocked, providing free drinks, snacks, and perhaps even free gasoline to the store's patrons, which grew to include most of the population of West Asheville before the night was over.

The Brahma bull arrived at the club and found the couple on the dance floor getting down to the sound of George Michael's top ten hit "Too Funky." To this day, George Michael's songs remind me of this fight call. The confrontation quickly went from verbal to physical. Tables were knocked over, drinks were spilled, and the ex-boyfriend was hauled out to the parking lot, where I arrived a few minutes later.

Later in court, he stood before the judge with his attorney and explained all this including the detail that she was now his ex-fiancé. He had, of course, been fired from his job for leaving the convenience store unattended.

After hearing the story, the judge gave the defendant a 10-minute lecture and ordered him to attend anger-management classes and pay restitution to the club for damages and to me for my broken glasses. He was placed on probation to ensure this happened. Losing his job made the repayment part of his punishment difficult. For over a year, I received a check of $10 to $20 every month from the court clerk for my share of the restitution.

Unfortunately, property damage warrants taken out by the club for his ex-fiancé's ex-boyfriend were not served as the man never returned to Asheville. I sometimes wonder, 30 years later, how many of those involved remember the incident. I won't forget it. That ride across the parking lot was an experience that remains unmatched in my law enforcement career.

RSL

8. Peter Smith: A Controversial Hanging

Peter Smith addresses the crowd before his hanging. October 2, 1905, Marshall, N.C. (UNC Libraries: Public Domain).

"Most men fear getting laughed at or humiliated by a romantic prospect while most women fear rape and death." — Gavin de Becker, American author, and security specialist.

On Tuesday night, November 8, 1904, Mayo Reeves and Lyda Wells were out hunting for possums and raccoons in Spring Creek, N.C. That Tuesday was election day, incumbent President Theodore Roosevelt retained the presidency, and Robert Glenn was elected N.C. governor. No one in Madison County knew it at that time, but the election's outcome would seal the fate of one of its residents and save the life of another.

Around midnight, Reeves and Wells sat down, waiting for their dogs to return to them and preparing to head home, when they heard what sounded like "a woman hollering." Moments later, a distraught, out-of-breath, 15-year-old Eva Suttles, emerged from the darkness. Her dress was muddy and wet. Wells rose to his feet, and she grabbed him. She appeared to be terrified.

> *"Eva Suttles came running and said Peter Smith was up there trying to kill her, and she wanted us to take her home," Reeves said.*

Thus began a convoluted and sometimes confusing tale that began with the unsolved murder of a pregnant teenager and ended with a walk to the gallows.

Instead of taking Eva Suttles home, Reeves and Wells took her to the nearest house, Jesse Seigle's home and all of them spent the night there.

Eva's Night of Terror

In her testimony in Superior Court, Eva said that she had gotten up in the night to visit the outhouse wearing only her night clothes and stockings. On her way back to the house, she encountered Smith standing in front of the door. He had the satchel in which Eva kept her Sunday clothes as well as her shoes, which he had apparently retrieved by entering the house and getting them from under her bed. She said that Smith had been to her house several times and knew where she kept her things. He also had a gun, which she said "might have been longer than my arm."

When she told Smith she was going to call her father for help, he put his hand over her mouth. Then, with his gun hand around her waist. He put the satchel over her arm. He took her to the top of the hill at Sol Gentry's field, about 200 yards from the house. Once there, he allowed her to dress and put on her shoes.

They traveled about two miles to Nathan Woody's field. She ran and climbed a fence, but he caught her, pulled her off the fence, and violently threw her to the ground. It was here that Smith raped her for the first time.

> "I made a break for liberty and got nearly to the top of the fence. The prisoner (Smith) caught me and jerked me flat on my back and used me as he pleased," Eva said.

From there, they traveled to the first ford of John's Branch above Jesse Seigle's house, about three miles from her home, where he raped her again. She testified that she was raped twice between the field and the ford but could not be certain where those assaults took place.

At the ford, he clubbed her in the head twice. She wasn't sure if he used his gun or a club the first time. The second blow glanced off her head and hit her shoulder blade.

> "I think he hit me with the gun the second time. I could see lightning when he struck me," Eva said.

Smith dragged her along the road for a distance that she estimated to be the width of the Madison County courthouse. He attempted to cut her throat, but in the dark, he mistakenly used the back of the blade instead of the edge, leaving a three-and-a-half-inch red mark across her throat.

> "After he struck me (in the head) the second time, I ran and got to Wells and Reeves. The prisoner pursued me," Eva said. "He caught my dress once and pulled it nearly off. I caught it up and ran towards Seigle's house. It was not very far away. I did not know that Reeves and Wells were down the road."

At some point, Eva lost the satchel. She thought she slung it off her arm during her final dash, but she was unsure.

A Tolerably Thin Story

Peter Smith seems to have gone directly from the ford of John's Branch to his nephew W.R. "Riley" Smith's home, arriving between midnight and daybreak. Riley testified that Peter was carrying his gun and Eva's satchel when he arrived. Peter asked Riley for some supper and requested that he go let out Peter's 11-year-old son, whom he had locked in the cabin before leaving that evening.

Peter Smith told Riley his version of the night's events.

He was at home in bed, asleep, as was his son. His wife was away helping someone with a sick child. He was awakened by someone yelling and stepping on the porch. He got up, lit a lamp, and opened the door to find a man standing there. The stranger wanted Smith to show him the way to Chestnut Gap and was willing to pay him $1 to do so. Smith declined, but the man was insistent, and he finally agreed to go with him.

Here is Smith's entire description of the man from his trial testimony:

> *"He was a tolerably thin man with striped clothes on.*
> *He was tolerably young. He said he lived in Haywood.*
> *I asked his name. He kept talking and did not tell me."*

He gave Smith a satchel to carry, which Smith believed belonged to the man. They found Eva Suttles sitting on a log beside the road, apparently waiting for them. The man took Eva by the hand, and they continued on their way. When they came to the ford of John's Branch above Jesse Seigle's house, Smith blundered into something in the dark or lost his footing and got hurt. At this point, Smith stated that he was going home, and since he had come halfway, he demanded to be paid half the $1 fee. The man was unwilling to pay and called Smith a "son of a bitch with an oath to it."

Smith stepped forward and clubbed the man with his gun. He told Riley that the man and the girl were standing close together, hand in hand, in the dark, and he was afraid he had hit the girl by mistake.

Between the night of November 8 and his arrest, Smith also told essentially this same story to his brother-in-law, Vance Ledford, and J.P. "John" Plemmons. In both accounts and his trial testimony, Smith stated that the man shot at him with what he thought was a .22-caliber pistol. Curiously, he did not mention being shot at to his nephew. Reeves testified that he and Wells were about 100 yards from the ford and did not hear any shots. Smith also told Plemmons that when he stuck the man or possibly Eva, he "knocked the rib off his little rifle gun."

Around daybreak, Eva's father, Alexander Suttles, arrived at the Seigle house. He had awakened early, found Eva missing, and had gone looking for her. After asking Eva why she went missing and hearing her explanation of the night's events, he briefly searched for the missing satchel, then took Eva to two Justices of the Peace (one was out of blank warrants), swore out a warrant against Peter Smith and placed it in the hands of a deputy sheriff. Then they returned home, and he sent for a physician to examine her. Alexander wasted no time getting this matter before a judge and jury.

That same morning, on his way home, Reeves noticed signs of a struggle and blood along the road.

> *"I went back down the road the next morning," he said. "I saw where people had been scuffling around and a heap of blood along the road. It was scattered along the road from about where the girl came to us, back to the ford of the branch."*

That afternoon, Alexander Suttles retrieved Eva's satchel from a ridge about 200 yards from Riley Smith's home. Peter Smith had hung it on a sapling there and shared its location with Riley, who went with Suttles to get it. Volunteers from the community fanned out and searched the mountains and woods for Smith.

The Elusive Peter Smith

Smith's explanation for why he did not return home was that he was afraid the man he struck with his gun might come looking for him. His next stop was Vance Ledford's house, where he spent Wednesday night. He briefly returned home Thursday evening, ate supper, learned from his wife that men were hunting him, and left after dark. He claimed that this was when he learned he was being charged with rape. Smith bedded down in a fence corner that night. Friday, he traveled to Bailey Plemmons' house to collect fruit he was promised for a day's work. He stayed the night, and this is where a five-man posse found and arrested him on Saturday. Smith was carrying a gun and a knife when captured.

On Sunday morning, four days after the assault, Dr. T.J. "Tom" Frisbee examined Eva. He found "a right smart-sized knot on the left side of her head" and a bruise about the size of a dollar on her left shoulder blade. The doctor did a thorough investigation, including having Eva remove her clothing, inspecting her genitals, and even introducing a speculum into her vagina.

> "I had Eva remove clothes from her person for me to examine. There were splotches of blood on them and dried spots that indicated dried semen or the seminal discharge from the male. In addition to external genital organs being swollen, they were covered with dried blood. The hair was matted. Her condition indicated to me that some violence had been done to her."

Dr. Frisbee testified at the Justice of the Peace hearing that day and at Smith's trial in March.

Smith was brought before Justice of the Peace, J. F. Askew, at Freizeland School for a preliminary hearing and bound over to be tried during the next term of Madison County Superior Court in February. The public sentiment was against Smith. Both Jasper Ebbs and L. C. Plemmons testified to overhearing talk of lynching Smith both before and during the hearing.

> *"I was one of a party of five who searched for the defendant and arrested him on Saturday," said Plemmons. "They said if they found him, and he resisted, they would kill him. They said he ought to be lynched. This was (the talk) around the schoolhouse on the day he was tried before the Justice of the Peace."*

Peter Smith and his brother, John, talked Jasper Ebbs into representing Peter at the hearing. Ebbs was a well-respected community member, had been a Justice of the Peace and was a prominent member of the county school board. It is important to note here that Jasper was not an attorney. He was just a neighbor helping out a neighbor. Regardless, this appeared to be a smart move on the Smiths part, but it would backfire with devastating results at the trial.

Too Many Versions of the Truth

Peter Smith's trial began on Monday, March 6, 1905. Judge Fred Moore presided, Solicitor Mark W. Brown prosecuted, and Attorney I.N. "Isaac Newton" Ebbs represented Smith. I.N. Ebbs called his brother, Jasper, as a defense witness.

The story Smith told Jasper had one compelling difference from the stories he told his nephew, brother-in-law, and John Plemmons. In this version, the stranger hired Smith to go get Eva and then guide her and the man to Chestnut Gap.

> *"He consented to the contract (with the man) and went over somewhere toward Suttle's and met the girl over*

there toward Suttle's house. He said she had everything ready. I mean, she had her satchel and things in it," Ebbs said.

"(Smith) said he went to Suttle's house or near his house, and there met the girl and carried her on (his) back till he got up on John's branch. He said the man was there sitting by the road. He said he wanted (the man) to pay him, and they got into some dispute."

This final version of Smith's story that the unknown man had sent him to the Suttles home to get Eva and bring her to him was the point where a smoldering pile of Smith's inconsistencies and untruths ignited and burned his testimony to the ground.

The three-day trial ended with the jury finding Smith guilty of rape but not guilty of abducting Eva from her home by force. The jury asked the court to show mercy, but unfortunately for Peter Smith in North Carolina in 1905, there was only one punishment for rape: death by hanging.

The Horrible Fate of Hannah Plemmons

The evidence and testimony of Peter Smith's trial lie entirely in the shadow of the disappearance of Hannah Plemmons. She was Peter Smith's stepdaughter. She went missing in early October of 1901; a month later, her head was found near the house where they lived. Her body was never recovered. Various sources have her as 15-17 years old when she died.

Hannah had a bad reputation, and there were rumors that she was pregnant. An article in the November 16 Asheville Register says she was at one point sent to live with the Christian Workers, a group of northern missionaries. The 1900 Census shows her living at the Wales Industrial School in Little Pine Creek Township and gives her age as 14.

(Editor's Note: For some reason, every contemporary newspaper account we found misidentifies her as Hannah Fleming, although they clearly identify Peter Smith as her stepfather.)

From the November 13, 1901, Charlotte News:

> *"On Thursday last, the head of the unfortunate girl, Hannah Fleming, was found about a quarter of a mile above Smith's house among a lot of logs. Hair and blood stains were found above the fence and at the foot of the hill, the head and some wearing apparel. The body of the unfortunate girl has not yet been discovered."*

The same article states that Smith is suspected to be "the author of the girl's downfall."

Peter Smith was arrested on November 9 for Hannah's murder and remained in jail until the next term of court; however, the grand jury did not indict him, so technically, he was never tried for this crime.

The most chilling portion of Eva Suttle's testimony referenced Hannah's death:

> *"He (Peter Smith) said after he got me killed, he was going to come and use me as a wife till I rotted. He said he was going to kill me that night and go back the next night and get my sister ... that he and another man killed his own wife's daughter ... he and the other man used her four times apiece during the night and killed her to keep her from telling it on them. I begged him not to kill me."*

There are some disturbing parallels between the death of Hannah Plemmons and the rape of Eva Suttles. In his book, *Until He Is Dead*:

Capital Punishment in the Western North Carolina History, former district attorney James Thomas Rusher notes:

> *"Smith testified that he "fastened" his ten-year-old son alone in his log cabin when he made the decision to accompany the stranger to the top of the mountain. One has to wonder about the propriety of doing this and what manner of man would do so.*
>
> *"This question becomes more perplexing when one realizes that on the night Hannah Plemmons (Smith's stepdaughter) was first missing, Peter Smith's wife was not at home, and Smith, on that night, locked his little son in the home."*

This brings us back to the mark on Eva's throat, which both she and Dr. Frisbee described in trial testimony.

> *"I noticed a red mark three- to three-and-a-half inches long around her neck," Frisbee said. "It was scarlet red, but there was no abrasion. She told me that the prisoner (Peter Smith) tried to cut her throat but had the back of the knife turned to (her) throat."*

Another unique aspect of the February 1905 term of Madison County Superior Court was that two men were tried and convicted for rape. In addition to Smith, Charlie Stines was convicted of raping Sarah Collins, who lived just outside Hot Springs. Both were sentenced to be hanged on May 12. Neither would swing on that day.

Both Smith and Stines appealed to the North Carolina Supreme Court. The court found no error in either case and upheld the convictions. This would seem to settle matters. However, both cases still had some twists and turns left to play out.

A Most Unusual Interview

On September 18, Eva was summoned to Solicitor Mark Brown's office in Asheville. I.N. Ebbs, Smith's defense attorney, had written to Governor Glenn saying that he had heard a rumor that Eva had admitted to falsely testifying against Smith under orders from her father. Glenn was attending the state fair in Concord, N.H. He wired a 10-day respite for Smith, which may have been a first, and directed Judge Moore and Solicitor Brown to question Eva regarding her testimony.

They asked her 11 questions. They made it clear to her that what she told them had life-and-death consequences for Peter Smith. Not only were the questions and answers typed up and sent to the governor, but the Asheville Citizen also published them the next day. Here are the four questions most important to our examination of the case from the newspaper account.

Interrogatory third: Miss Suttles, on your answers to the following questions depends the life or death of Peter Smith, and I warn you to be careful about all you say. State whether you testified on the trial of Peter Smith at Marshall was the truth.

Answer: It was the truth.

Fourth Interrogatory: Do you want to vary or change your testimony, as given there, in any respect?

Answer: No sir, I do not.

Fifth Interrogatory: Have you ever made an affidavit in which you stated that any part of your testimony, in that case, was false.

Answer: No sir, I have not.

*Sixth Interrogatory: Have you ever stated to any
person that any part of your testimony on that trial was
false?*

Answer: No sir.

We will skip the questions about whether she was a virtuous woman
before and after the assault, where she had been living, etc.

Pardons, Commutations and Respites

Smith appealed to the governor for a commutation of his sentence to life
in prison, but both Judge Moore and Solicitor Brown positively refused
to recommend it. From Governor Glenn's statement:

> *"After carefully reading all the testimony, and while
> part of the prosecutrix's evidence is very much
> contradicted, still in many respects, she is strongly
> corroborated by creditable witnesses, especially the
> medical expert, whose testimony shows clearly, to my
> mind, that this outrage was perpetrated without the
> consent of the woman. The prisoner's own testimony
> was conflicting, contradictory. His flight, conduct, and
> character strongly tended to corroborate the State's
> testimony."*

Charlie Stines fared far better than Smith. Governor Glenn commuted his
sentence to life imprisonment on July 31, 1905. The same man, elected
on the day of Smith's crime, condemned Smith and spared Stines. The
next governor, William Walton Kitchin, granted Stines a pardon on June
9, 1911, noting that Glenn had promised to do so before he left office.

In Marshall on October 2, 1905, nearly a year after the crime, more than
1,000 people gathered to watch Peter Smith finally keep his appointment
with the hangman. Only 50 people were allowed to witness the
execution, which was held behind a screen.

At 12:30 p.m., Smith was brought out to an elevated platform where he addressed the crowd as seen in C.L. Brittain's well-known photo.

Smith's final words to those assembled were: "I am not guilty of the crime as charged against me. I am sick and can't talk anymore. Goodbye friends."

Smith was then taken back into the jail, where he dropped into a chair from exhaustion. At 1:00 pm, Madison County Sheriff Cole told him it was time to go. He was assisted from his chair and walked with the sheriff to the gallows. Two hymns were sung: "Sin Can Never Enter There" and "Is Thy Heart Right with God." Reverend L.B. Compton gave a bible reading and offered a prayer. At this point, Smith broke down and wept.

Cole was assisted in the execution by Buncombe County Sheriff Reed and Deputy White. They placed a black cap over Smith's head and adjusted the noose around his neck. Cole took his position at the lever. When released by Reed, who had been holding him steady, Smith staggered, slowly recovered, and was able to stand on his own. Reed gave the signal, and Cole pulled the lever. The trap sprung, the body fell, and a drop of six feet broke Smith's neck. No sign of struggle was visible. Five minutes later, Doctors Roberts and Jones pronounced Peter Smith dead.

Spurious Accusations

Before he was hanged, Peter Smith was allowed to speak with newspaper reporters and made a statement regarding the death of Hannah Plemmons. In his book, Rusher quotes the Asheville Gazette News, which gave the fullest report of Smith's remarks:

> *"He said that Henry and Columbus Frisbee carried*
> *the girl into the woods and cut her throat. He did not*
> *state how he knew this. He did say, however, that Jim*

and Ben Allison would swear that (the Frisbees) cut the girl's throat."

Multiple newspapers noted that Sheriff Reed thought Smith's statement to be false and made for the purpose of getting a commutation of his sentence.

Rusher takes issue with the idea that Allison would give testimony favorable to Peter Smith and quotes the affidavit Allison swore for Smith's arrest in 1901 for Hannah Plemmons' murder as proof.

> *"State of North Carolina, County of Madison. James Allison personally appeared before me a Justice of the Peace of Madison County and, after being duly sworn deposes and says that on or about the 7th day of October 1901, one Peter Smith did to the best of said plaintiff's belief willfully and maliciously murder and kill and conceal Hannah Plemmons contrary to law in such cases and against the peace and dignity of the State."*

The Case for Not Guilty

The case for Peter Smith not being guilty boils down to three main arguments. He could not have possibly carried, dragged, or somehow kept possession of Eva Suttles while traveling at least two miles (probably more) over some of the most difficult terrain in Madison County. There is no way a man his age could not have been physically able to rape Eva four times in the space of one evening. And finally, he never confessed to the crime and would not have gone to eternity with a lie on his lips.

These arguments are far from insurmountable. Let's take each in turn. How did he carry her off? He didn't. He tricked her into going with him. The most probable theory, chronicled in the September 9 News and Observer and other papers, was that Eva had a sweetheart that Smith knew about and convinced her that he would help her elope. It's important to remember that most probable does not equal true. He may well have come up with a different ruse.

From the October 5, 1905, Wadesboro Messenger and Intelligencer:

> *"It is believed by those who attended the trial and who heard all the testimony that Smith committed the crime, although he did not drag the girl to the mountains. It is believed that Smith had the afternoon before told Eva Suttles that her lover awaited her across the mountain that night and that for her to come and marry him, that Smith was to escort her across the mountains. It is also thought that the girl met Smith outside the house and that after getting her to the mountains, he committed the crime."*

No one believed Eva's account of her abduction from her home. The jury found Smith not guilty of carrying her off by force and guilty of raping her. Dr. Frisbee's examination and testimony left no doubt that she had been raped. Smith, by his own admission was out that night and traveling with her. He had her satchel when he visited his nephew later that night.

It is not impossible that he raped her four times. It is also possible that a scared teenage girl who was raped slammed into the ground, struck on the head multiple times, and had to run for her life misremembered some of the details. Also, one or more of the assaults may not have been sexual intercourse. Finally, Smith may have had an accomplice who Suttles did not name out of fear or some other reason.

Interestingly, after her interview with Judge Moore and Solicitor Brown in Asheville, in which she confirmed her trial testimony against Smith, Eva refused to stay at the hotel they offered and insisted on being locked in the county jail. Since Smith was securely locked in jail, one can't help but wonder who she was afraid of.

The Credible Case for Guilty

Smith's story of his activities and movements that night and the time between his arrest is problematic at best. His accounts of a man no one else saw, shots no one else heard, and his admission that he might have accidentally clubbed Eva with his gun are ludicrous.

Every witness at his trial who was asked about Smith's character stated that it was bad or bad as far as women were concerned. His admission that he was accused of raping another woman and his arrest for the murder of his stepdaughter three years earlier doesn't inspire confidence either.

Did they hang an innocent man? No, Peter Smith was many things, but innocent wasn't one of them. In our opinion, if Reeves and Wells had not been out hunting on the night of November 8, this would not be a story about Peter Smith and the controversy over his guilt or innocence. It would be a story about the disappearance of Eva Suttles or whether Peter Smith was Western North Carolina's first known serial killer.

Epilogue

Eva Suttles married Patton "Nugent" Leeper, a butcher, in Knox County, TN, in 1907. She gave birth to three children: Rosa, Patton James, and Hazel Amber Leeper. Eva died in 1981 at the age of 91.

My Introduction to the Peter Smith Controversy

If you grew up in Madison County sooner or later, you heard about the case of Peter Smith and probably saw the photograph of him addressing the crowd from the roof of a shed at the county seat of Marshall in 1905, right before they took him behind a partition and carried out his execution.

I first heard the story as a teenager after seeing the photo at Joe's Junque, a secondhand store on Main Street in Marshall. I went there with my best friend, who scoured this establishment for secondhand paperback books, including the works of John D. MacDonald, Louis L'Amour, and some more questionable series of novels revolving around extraordinary martial arts skills and vigilante justice.

One of Joe's classified ads from the Asheville-Citizen Time read: "Antiques – Odds, ends, 3,000 Indian artifacts, Joe's Junque, Main Street, Marshall, N.C., Closed Wednesday and Sunday." It gives you a bit of a feel for his establishment. The Indian artifacts were mostly arrowheads; I believe he donated them to Mars Hill University at some point.

It is incredible how events that happened generations in the past find people in the most peculiar times and places and create lifelong memories.

RSL

9. Murderous Manhunts: Will Harris and Broadus Miller

Pack Square with Vance Monument 1910 by H.W. Pelton
(LOC: Public Domain).

"Those who wish to be feared seem to forget humanity's tendency to kill those they fear." — *Wayne Gerard Trotman, British independent filmmaker, writer, and composer.*

If you have taken one of the Asheville ghost tours, you will be familiar with the story of the man who called himself Will Harris and his murderous shooting spree that took place on November 13, 1906. Before the city removed the Vance Monument, a 19th-century granite obelisk, from Pack Square in 2021, tour guides would point out a spot where one of Harris' bullets nicked its base. It's said that a young Thomas Wolfe used to climb the fence and touch this indentation.

Harris, a drunken Black man armed with a .303 Savage lever-action rifle, killed two white policemen and three Black citizens in the space of 20 minutes on that cold and snowy night and then fled. A massive manhunt was launched and ended two days later in nearby Fletcher when a posse caught up to him and shot him an estimated 100 times.

At the inquest two days later, Sheriff Wallace of Mecklenburg County could not be certain if the man was Harris. Squire J. P. Hunter of Charlotte was positive the man was not Harris, the notorious Mecklenburg County outlaw and escaped convict. One man suggested he was Rufe Lindsey of York, S.C., but no one was ever truly confident of the marauding shooter's identity.

This terrifying night made a strong impression on Wolfe, still considered North Carolina's greatest writer, who was six years old at the time and lived nearby. In fact, his 1937 short story, *"The Child by Tiger,"* was inspired by it, and the actions of the story's protagonist, Dick Prosser, a Black manservant, mirror those of Harris.

Prosser is respected and liked by the community, but he hides a dark side. The character snaps and goes on a killing spree with a rifle. Later, cornered by a mob, he is shot almost 300 times. There are many parallels between the events of Wolfe's story and Harris' rampage. Both men had been drinking but displayed almost uncanny marksmanship; someone continuously rang the town's fire bell as a warning, and a hardware store was emptied of guns to arm the crowd.

The story ends with the point-of-view character, only referred to as Spangler, attempting to make sense of the night's events and reconcile how one person can have so much good and so much evil within them at the same time. How a man can be "two worlds together: a tiger and a child."

The Era of Jim Crow and Lynchings

Just as Asheville has its ghost tour, Morganton has a ghost walk. And if you have taken it, you have doubtless heard about the brutal 1927 murder of Gladys Kincaid, a 15-year-old hosiery mill worker, and the man accused of killing her, Broadus Miller, a 23-year-old Black construction worker.

One of the more positive aspects of ghost tours is that they teach the history of a place and tell stories that help explain the actions and motivations of the people who lived in that place and time. Sometimes, this also gives visitors a sense of the cultural forces, customs, and laws that produced a set of outcomes or continue to deliver those outcomes. Many factors that shaped Will Harris' fate played out again about 20 years later and 60 miles farther east in the almost two-week-long manhunt for Broadus Miller.

Jim Crow laws brought racial segregation to the country from the end of Reconstruction around 1880 to the civil rights movement in the 1950s. These laws affected many parts of daily life, requiring separate public and private facilities for Blacks and whites.

An 1889 North Carolina law decreed that textbooks were not interchangeable between white and Black schools but would continue to be used by the race that first used them. Other states had separate textbooks for white and nonwhite students. Railroads had to provide separate passenger cars, waiting rooms, and even ticket windows. A Nebraska law made marriages void if one party was white and the other was one-eighth or more Black, Japanese, or Chinese.

Some states made it illegal for whites and Blacks to work in the same room, and factories had to have separate entrances. Separate washrooms were required in mines. Blacks were given the right to vote by the 15th Amendment in 1870, and the Civil Rights Act of 1875 outlawed race-based discrimination in jury selection, but all manner of tactics were used to avoid compliance with these laws.

From 1882 to 1968, there were 160 lynchings, or illegal executions by mobs, in South Carolina (156 Black and 4 white) and 101 in North Carolina (86 Black and 15 white). These numbers come from the Tuskegee Institute, which is now Tuskegee University. It's important to note that these are just the lynchings that we know about.

This was the environment in which Miller grew up. He was born about 1904 in Greenwood County, S.C., which had the most lynchings in the state, according to the Equal Justice Initiative (EJI). Miller would have been about two years old when Harris went on his killing spree in Asheville. His early life was hardscrabble. Orphaned, he and his three siblings were taken in by Thomas and Alpha Walker, Black sharecroppers.

In January of the year that Miller was born, a mob lynched a Black man known as "General" Lee in Reevesville, S.C., for allegedly knocking on the door of a white woman's house. Lee was arrested and charged with criminally assaulting a white woman. He was identified by distinctive tracks left by his "leggings" and by a pair of "homemade knucks" found nearby. A mile outside of Reevesville, a mob of about 50 white men seized him from police officers who were transporting him by buggy. Two days later, Lee was found tied to a tree and shot to death.

In 1916, when Miller was about 13, a mob in Abbeville, S.C., about 15 miles east of Greenwood, lynched Anthony Crawford, a prosperous Black farmer, for arguing with a white shopkeeper over cotton prices. Crawford was abducted from jail, beaten, and dragged through the Black section of town. He was taken to the fairgrounds, and although he was most likely already dead, he was hung from a tree, and his body was riddled with bullets.

Who Killed Essie Walker?

In 1920, at the age of 16, Miller left home and moved to nearby Anderson, S.C., where he lived in a boarding house. He was probably seeking employment other than as a field laborer. About nine months later, he was accused, tried, and convicted of killing Essie Walker, a middle-aged Black woman who may have been his landlady.

On the evening of Sunday, May 1, 1921, Walker's grandson, Bob, discovered her body lying on the hallway floor of her boarding house on West Market Street in Anderson. We do not know the exact time the body was found, but it was after dark because he had to summon a policeman with a flashlight to find out what was blocking the door.

County physician Dr. Halbert H. Acker, Jr. examined Essie Walker's body and found two skull fractures and fractures of the bones on the left side of her face. Additionally, the lower third of the left arm and the left middle finger were fractured. Finally, Acker noted a bullet wound in her right chest in the second rib space with extensive powder burns. The bullet had ranged downward, going through the heart, liver, stomach, and left kidney before logging just beneath the skin in the small of her back.

Based on documents from the South Carolina Archives and Dr. Kevin W. Young's dissertation, "The World of Broadus Miller: Homicide, Lynching, and Outlawry in Early Twentieth-Century North and South Carolina," here is a summary of the events that led up to Walker's death and Miller's conviction.

On the morning of her death, Ben Anderson, her grandson Bob, Jim Mattison, and Broadus Miller had breakfast with Essie Walker at the boarding house. The next day, Monday, in a signed statement, Miller says that he saw Mattison beat Walker with a bat and then shoot her with a .32-caliber pearl-handled revolver that had been stored in her wardrobe.

A week after the killing, Jim Mattison and Broadus Miller were indicted. Two weeks after the murder, Miller was tried for the crime, and Mattison testified for the prosecution. There were reports in two South Carolina newspapers that Miller had bloodstains on his clothing after the killing, but there is no mention of this in the S.C. Archives materials, and it seems it would have been persuasive to the jury at his trial. If true, however, it would be another similarity to the crime he would be accused of in Morganton, N.C., six years later.

Judge George E. Prince had concerns about Miller's sanity and ordered Dr. Ann Young, a psychiatrist, to examine the defendant. She concluded that Broadus Miller "was not normal mentally" and testified at Miller's trial that his mental condition made him "irresponsible for the crime." An all-white jury was deadlocked and could not reach a verdict, so Judge Prince declared a mistrial.

While in jail awaiting a new trial, Miller agreed to plead guilty to manslaughter and was sentenced to three years in the state penitentiary in Columbia.

Whether Miller killed Essie Walker, assisted Jim Mattison in her murder, or just witnessed the crime, it must have been a pivotal and traumatic event in the teenager's life. Did this episode set in motion the eventual murder of Gladys Kincaid in Morganton six years later? We will never know.

> *"A middle-aged Black woman had been brutally killed; the 17-year-old African American accused of killing her received a three-year prison sentence. Six years later, the same individual would be accused of killing a white girl; he would then be targeted by thousands of armed manhunters and pursued throughout western North Carolina. The contrasting reactions are striking but hardly surprising,"* Dr. Young wrote in "The World of Broadus Miller."

Miller was discharged from the S.C. State Penitentiary on May 31, 1924, two years and eight months after entering the prison. In the intervening years, the boll weevil had come to South Carolina, devastating the cotton crop and causing his family to resettle in Asheville.

During the Roaring 20s, Asheville experienced its greatest building boom, with the construction of new residential neighborhoods and landmarks like the Jackson Building, City Building, Buncombe County Courthouse, Grove Arcade, and Battery Park. The city was nicknamed the Paris of the South.

His adoptive parents, the Walkers, had found work there: Thomas as a construction worker and Alpha as a maid. They lived in a Black neighborhood on the south side of Pack Square. Miller followed them there, and on June 30, 1924, he married 18-year-old Mamie Wadlington at the Buncombe County courthouse.

Assault Accusations Lead to Violence

As economic forces moved more Blacks to Asheville, racial tensions increased. When several assault or rape allegations against Black men by white women surfaced from August through October 1925, these tensions reached their breaking point. The two most prominent cases were those of Alvin Mansel of Pickens, S.C., and Preston Neely of Laurens, S.C., requiring the National Guard to provide security for two extraordinary back-to-back trials.

In August, a white woman reported being assaulted on Sunset Mountain by a Black man. On the morning of Saturday, September 19, a second woman claimed that she had been attacked at the same location. She described her attacker as a tall, light-skinned Black man in his thirties. The police arrested 17-year-old Mansel, a kitchen worker at Fairview Cottage, a nearby tuberculosis sanatorium.

On the afternoon that the crime was committed, Sheriff E. M. Mitchell arrived at the woman's hospital room with Mansel, another Black man, and three deputies. She immediately identified Mansel as the man who had assaulted her.

According to North Carolina Supreme Court records, she testified that he had passed her while she was walking home alone that morning, and a few minutes later, he came back with a rock in his hand and used it to strike her and knock her down. At some point, she lost consciousness. When she woke up, her assailant was gone.

Once word spread about Mansel's arrest, a mob began to form in Asheville. That night, around 11:00 p.m., a mob estimated at between 500 and 1,000 men converged on the Buncombe County jail. According to an article in the Sunday, September 20, Asheville Citizen, they broke through the gates and searched the building for the accused, going cell-to-cell and holding lights up to the faces of each prisoner. They even checked the coal bins to see if he had been hidden there.

Unable to find Mansel in the jail, some of the mob went to Sheriff Mitchell's house, and around 300 traveled to nearby Hendersonville to check the jail there. If Michell had not had the foresight to move Mansel to Charlotte, the prisoner would have surely died at the hands of the mob.

Preston Neely's story mirrors Mansel's in most respects. On Thursday afternoon, October 22, a white woman in West Asheville reported that a Black man had assaulted her. According to an article in the October 27 Asheville Citizen, she said the man pulled a revolver and threatened to kill her if she uttered a word.

On Tuesday, October 26, police arrested Neely, a dishwasher at the Moxley Sandwich shop, after his accuser recognized him in Woolworth's on Patton Avenue and followed him on the street until she got the attention of Officer W. C. Glenn, who was stationed at the Post Office. He intercepted Neely at the corner of Patten Avenue and Grove Street by commandeering a bus. Once news of the arrest spread, another mob formed, and again, Sheriff Mitchell had to move the prisoner, this time to Raleigh, for his safety.

During the first week of November, Mansel and Neely were brought back to Asheville for trial. A detachment of National Guard soldiers was stationed at the jail and stood guard in the courtroom during the trial, armed with Springfield rifles. Judge A. M. Stack ordered every person entering the courtroom to be searched. Reports suggest that as many as 700 spectators were present.

The November 4 News & Observer describes the prisoners' accommodations.

> *"Mansel and Neely are confined in the death cell, which is in the basement of the jail. The cell is a massive steel cage, built independently of walls and floors, being a complete steel unit in itself."*

Despite the testimony of multiple sanatorium workers regarding his whereabouts on the day of the crime, Mansel was quickly found guilty and sentenced to die in the electric chair. When Judge Stack asked him if he had anything to say, Mansel is reported to have replied:

> *"I hope to meet you all in heaven. I am not guilty, but the jury has come out and said I was."*

The North Carolina Supreme Court upheld Mansel's conviction, but his death sentence was later commuted to life in prison by Governor Angus W. McLean, and five years later, in 1930, he received a pardon from Governor Max Gardner.

Preston Neely's trial began shortly after Sheriff Mitchell escorted Mansel from the courtroom. To everyone's surprise, Neely was found not guilty. Minutes after the verdict was read, Neely was escorted out of the courtroom by 50 National Guardsmen with fixed bayonets. The prosecutor and judge indicated that the accused was being "remanded to jail" for further investigation. In reality, Neely was placed in a police convoy and taken to an undisclosed location in South Carolina, where he was released.

The Murder of Gladys Kincaid

Sometime in 1925, Miller returned to Greenwood County. On March 2, 1926, he was arraigned for housebreaking and larceny for an attempt to burglarize a clothing store owned by Louis Mark, a Russian-born Jewish immigrant. Miller pled guilty and was sentenced to a year on the chain gang.

After serving ten months "on the county roads," he returned to Asheville in the spring of 1927 and was hired by contractor and stone mason Dante Martin as a construction worker for a project in Morganton, building the Franklin Pierce Tate House, a two-story Colonial Revival style mansion. A native of Italy, Martin had arrived in the United States in 1913. He arrived in Asheville in 1922.

Tate was a prominent Morganton banker and mill owner and the son of Confederate Colonel Samuel McDowell Tate. The mansion was listed on the National Register of Historic Places in 1986.

Miller, his wife, and other members of Martin's construction crew moved into Will Berry's boardinghouse on Bouchelle Street, a short distance from the worksite.

Around this time, 15-year-old Gladys Kincaid took a job at Garrou Knitting Mill. Her father had died of influenza four years earlier. She had dropped out of school and gone to work to help support her mother and seven siblings. Her daily mile-and-a-half walk from home to work down Bouchelle Street took her past the boardinghouse.

On Tuesday, June 21, 1927, about three weeks after Miller began his stay in Morganton, Kincaid got off work at the mill at 5:30 p.m. and started her long walk home. Gladys Kincaid paused along the way to chat with Ida Whisenant, who was outside in her yard with her children. After a brief conversation, she continued on her way home to prepare supper for her family, who were working on the farm.

According to newspaper accounts, Whisenant noticed a Black man wearing a yellow raincoat and carrying a length of iron pipe passing by just before she spoke with Kincaid. The June 24, Greensboro Daily News said Whisenant recalled remarking at the time that "He is well protected against mad dogs."

Around 7:00 p.m., Kincaid's mother, Mary Jane Kincaid, came in from the fields and noticed Gladys was not home. The family went out searching for Gladys. Her brother, Harvey Kincaid, and his friend, Virgil Fox, heard a groan and found her unconscious in some brush a few yards from the road, about 500 yards from Whisenant's house. She was bleeding from a head wound, and the back of her skull had been "crushed like an eggshell." A bloody iron pipe lay nearby. They flagged down a passing car and rushed her to Grace Hospital. According to her death certificate, Gladys Kincaid died at 3:30 a.m. the next day.

Miller quickly became a target of the investigation. After speaking with Whisenant, the police went to the boardinghouse, where they found Miller conspicuously absent and a bloodstained yellow raincoat hidden behind a door.

They arrested Miller's wife, Mamie, and Will Berry, the owner of the boardinghouse, as material witnesses. Mobs of angry white men gathered in Morganton with one thought: find and kill Broadus Miller.

News and Observer Reporter Frank Smethurst described the scene he found in Morganton that Tuesday night:

> *"Two thousand men went wild. Armed with every sort of weapon from ancient squirrel rifles to the latest automatic, they beat about the streets here, pried into alleys, backyards, and every conceivable hiding place, and then lay a dragnet far out into the hills."*

The case became a full-fledged media circus. In addition to Smethurst, newspapermen dispatched to Morganton included B. S. Griffith of the

Charlotte News, L. E. Cooper of the Asheville Times, and Johnston Avery, who represented both the Hickory Daily Record and the Associated Press.

Largest Manhunt in WNC History

For the next 12 days, the entire region descended into utter chaos. Sam Ervin, Jr., attorney for Burke County and future U.S. senator, described it as "the largest manhunt in western North Carolina history." During the search, Ervin served as a legal advisor to Sheriff J. J. "Jules" Hallyburton.

The manhunt would spread over three states: North Carolina, South Carolina, and Virginia. Black men were stopped, arrested, and detained until it could be undeniably determined that they were not Broadus Miller. Some of these encounters were life-threatening.

Dr. Young shared the following example in Blood in the Hills: A History of Violence in Appalachia.

> *"In the southern end of town, a mob of townspeople seized a worker walking home from his job in a local tannery. As they prepared to hang the man from a railroad bridge, one of his white coworkers—a man named Bert Walker—happened upon the scene. Insisting that the man had been at work all day and was not the suspect, Walker eventually persuaded the mob to release its intended victim. In the words of one press account, "If the [suspect] had been caught the first night after the crime, there would undoubtedly have been a necktie party."*

On Wednesday, June 22, Sheriff Hallyburton swore out an affidavit charging Miller with felony murder and rape. There was no evidence that Kincaid was raped, and multiple newspaper articles emphasized this.

The same day the sheriff put forth the affidavit, Burke County justices of the peace, George Battle and William Hallyburton, issued an official proclamation declaring Broadus Miller an outlaw. Immediately, Burke County approved a $250 reward for the fugitive, dead or alive, which the state of North Carolina matched. Local businesses and private individuals also pledged almost $1,500. Broadus Miller officially had a price on his head.

On Wednesday, June 22, a man matching Miller's description was seen at a store in Bridgewater near Lake James. Hundreds of men jumped into cars, raced to the area, and then on to Nebo, where it was thought Miller might have hopped a freight train.

The National Guard was deployed in Morganton for two days, Thursday and Friday, June 23 and 24, after Governor McLean reached out to Sheriff Hallyburton, who admitted to the governor that Miller would probably be lynched if caught.

Sightings and clues moved the searchers through the mountains as the trail ran hot and cold from Morganton to Nebo, Bridgewater, Adako, Collettsville, and Globe. Miller appears to have initially followed the Johns River northward from Morganton, so Nebo and Bridgewater were probably false sightings.

It began to look like Miller had managed to use the rugged terrain to elude his pursuers, but on the afternoon of Tuesday, June 28, he was spotted stealing milk and cornbread from Charlie Ingram's house on Cold Water Creek near Mortimer.

A report in the Thursday, June 30, Greensboro Daily News stated that a store in the Piney section near Globe was broken into and that a gun, some canned fruit, and a pair of shoes were stolen. Two paragraphs later, the story makes the following ominous statement:

"With the prevailing belief that Miller carries a gun for the first time in the six-day chase, members of the posse tonight are prepared to shoot without a great deal of provocation."

The chase came to an end on Sunday, July 3, on a wooded mountainside behind Concord United Methodist Church near Linville Falls, when 42-year-old Commodore Vanderbilt Burleson caught up with Miller and shot him dead.

Commodore was not a rank; it was Burleson's first name. One wonders what his friends called him. Burleson was a former Morganton town policeman, carpenter, building contractor, and, most notably, in this circumstance, an experienced bear hunter.

Burleson was also a member of the Morganton Klan and had been a member of the grand jury that recommended the state hospital and School for the Deaf stop hiring Black employees after Arthur Montague, a Black man, assaulted a deaf girl at the school in 1925. Both facts are documented in Dr. Young's "The World of Broadus Miller."

That Sunday morning, John Wiseman, coincidentally Burleson's uncle, discovered a cafe across the street from his general store in Linville Falls had been broken into, found a trail of discarded candy bar wrappers leading away from it, and called the Morganton police. A farmer in Ashford found a jar of milk missing from his springhouse, which was found empty a hundred yards away, and his daughter reported seeing a Black man with a gun cross the road at the church.

By this point, Miller was beyond physical and mental exhaustion. He was simply unable to cover his tracks after spending 12 days on the run, subsisting on whatever he could find or steal, sleeping on the ground, traveling through some of North Carolina's most challenging terrain, and facing relentless pursuit by men and bloodhounds.

Burleson was part of a party of four men, along with John Burnett, Fons Duckworth, and Harrison Pritchard, who had traveled to Linville Falls after hearing about the cafe break-in. Arriving at the church, the men split up and searched for the fugitive.

The men recognized Miller's distinctive footprints immediately. They had seen the same tracks a few days before trailing him in Caldwell County. Miller had worn out his shoes early in his flight and had been wrapping his raw, bloody feet in rags.

Gunshots End the Chase

Burleson said he pushed through some brush and found Miller sitting on a boulder. The fugitive fired at him with a 12-gauge shotgun, and he returned fire with his .45-caliber revolver, hitting Miller in the chest and mortally wounding him. A moment or two later, Miller closed his eyes and died.

There was some dispute regarding Burleson's account of the encounter. H.W. Gragg and Clyde Dula contended that Miller had been unarmed; they claimed to have tracked the fugitive for days, following him through dense laurel thickets, including places where it was necessary to crawl on hands and knees and had seen no sign that he had been carrying a gun.

Gragg suggested that Miller was shot while sleeping. Dula told reporters that he suspected Miller had been shot while surrendering, stating that the nature of the gunshot wound indicated Miller was shot with his hands in the air.

Burleson sued both men for slander. Gragg publicly apologized. Dula settled out of court with Burleson and agreed to pay one cent in damages. Shortly after this matter was settled, Burleson was sued by his companions, Burnett, Duckworth, and Pritchard, who wanted equal shares of the reward money.

Multiple newspapers carried stories of the gun battle between Burleson and Miller, and no two match. Here are three accounts of the shooting. All of the articles ran on page one of their respective papers on Monday, July 4.

Asheville Citizen went with: "Asheville Negro Fugitive Killed by Mountaineer:"

> *"The negro, according to the story told by Burleson and members of the posse who reached the scene a moment after the negro fell dead, was sitting on a boulder when Burleson unexpectedly walked up. The negro fired one shot from a shotgun. Burleson fired five times from a 45-calibre pistol as rapidly as he could pull the trigger. The last shot struck the negro below the heart, killing him instantly."*

Charlotte News reported: "Negro Outlaw Shot to Death in Mountains:"

> *"Burleson pushed ahead of the other members of his posse, and as he climbed over a rocky cliff, he came face to face with Miller. The negro cried "halt," and Burleson jumped behind a stump in time to save himself from a full load of shot, fired from a 12-gauge gun by the negro."*

> *"Burleson fired six times at the outlaw in that lonesome mountain duel, and the last shot struck Miller just below the heart. Men rushing up heard a groan, and the negro clutched at the wound in his side. When others arrived, he was dead."*

News & Observer stated: "Broadus Miller Meets his Doom in Gun Battle:"

> *"Raising the gun to his shoulder, he commanded*
> *Commodore Vanderbilt Burleson, a Morganton*
> *carpenter, to halt. Burleson advanced through the*
> *brush, and Miller fired. Instantly, Burleson fired back,*
> *and Miller, with a groan, pitched forward on his face*
> *dead, six gaping wounds showed through tattered rags*
> *that were his garments when he fled to the mountains*
> *before the infuriated citizens of Burke County nearly*
> *two weeks ago. Burleson was unhurt."*

Burleson and his three companions fastened a rope around Miller's legs and dragged him from the forest as if he were a deer or a bear. They placed the body in the backseat of Duckworth's Model T Ford and sped toward Morganton at breakneck speed. The descent down the mountain was reportedly more terrifying to Burleson than his confrontation with Miller.

On the way, they passed a car carrying Sheriff Hallyburton, Pardon Commissioner Edwin Bridges, and County Attorney Sam Ervin, Jr., who were rushing to the scene of the renewed manhunt. Governor McLean had dispatched Bridges to Morganton to assist Hallyburton and Ervin in preventing a lynching if Miller was caught.

News & Observer Reporter Ben Dixon MacNeill was in town when the Burleson posse arrived, and he described it as follows:

> *"An automobile swept into the Burke capital, with its*
> *siren shrieking. Four men rode in the car and over the*
> *right rear door projected the feet of a figure thrown*
> *carelessly on the floor. The feet were wrapped in rags.*
> *The left foot was partially bare and very Black. It hung*
> *loosely over the side of the car. The streets were filled*
> *with people going home from their places of worship.*

"Shooting half across the sidewalk before it was brought to a standstill, the car drew up before the courthouse. The rear door was opened, and two men grabbed the feet that projected. The body was dragged to the pavement, its head hitting sharply as it fell. For a moment, it lay there, with its red, gaping wounds in the naked breast and stomach still dripping. The clothing had almost all been torn off in his wandering through mountain forests.

"Again grasping the figure by the feet, two men dragged it across the sidewalk, across the courthouse lawn, pausing a moment before the door and then going in. A vast throng collected with miraculous speed. They yelled in exultation. Women embraced one another, and men shook one another by the hand and slapped one another on the back. Before the doors of the courthouse, they all clamored for a sight of the dead, naked fugitive."

So many individuals wanted to see the body and showed up, trying to gain access to the county building. The body was moved outside to the square and placed on the ground near the Burke County Confederate Monument, a nine-foot-tall statue of a soldier standing guard that was completed in 1918. More and more people continued to arrive, creating an almost carnival atmosphere.

Afraid that the situation might turn ugly, the police moved the body to the jail and brought Miller's wife and some of his coworkers to identify the body. Sheriff Hallyburton wanted to remove the body to an undertaking establishment, but as thousands of spectators arrived and demanded to see the body, he ordered it taken outside and laid on a board on the jailhouse steps. Officers roped off a path and allowed viewers to pass the body single file.

One man was arrested for kicking the corpse; some spectators spat on the body. By late afternoon, officials decided to put an end to the spectacle and took Miller's body back into the jail, put it into a coffin, and sent it by train to Statesville to be buried in an unmarked grave.

Commissioner Bridges and County Attorney Ervin immediately deposed Commodore Burleson and wrote a report for the governor. The shooting of Miller was found to be justified. However, other crimes committed while searching for Miller were not addressed. Beatings of Blacks accused of hiding Miller, damages to property, and fires were all overlooked and received little follow-up.

As the story of how Broadus Miller's body was treated and displayed, major newspapers ran editorials condemning the brutal maltreatment and perversion of justice. The Raleigh News condemned the display, running the headline, "Morganton Church-Goers Applaud a Gory Matinee." The Greensboro News quoted an AP reporter saying that more than 5,000 people were there that afternoon to view the remains and criticized "so many people... happily utilized a Sunday afternoon to drench themselves in savagery."

In an interesting turn of events, the next day, Monday, the 4th of July, was the Statesville Horse Show and a statewide rally for the Knights of the Ku Klux Klan of the Carolinas. An estimated 2,000 Klansmen gathered from all parts of North Carolina, South Carolina, Tennessee, and Virginia. Burleson was an honored guest, riding around the grandstands and in a parade that evening through the streets of Statesville.

The Ballads of Gladys Kincaid

The murder of Gladys Kincaid and the manhunt for Broadus Miller inspired a broadside poem and three folk ballads. In the weeks following the tragedy, amateur poets Henry D. Holsclaw and Harry Lee Pennell composed "The Murder of Gladys Kincaid," a narrative poem. Numerous residents of Burke County still have a broadside or a newspaper clipping from when the poem was published in a local newspaper.

The ballads include "The Dreadful Fate of Gladys Kincaid," "Gladys Kincaid," and "The Tragedy of Gladys Kincaid." Musicians Tim and Britt Poteat from Morganton wrote "The Dreadful Fate of Gladys Kincaid" in the fall of 1927. According to Dr. Young's article in the North Carolina Folklore Journal, they recorded the song, but the Kincaid family would not permit them to release the record.

The other two ballads were the work of unknown writers who set them to traditional folk melodies. By the early 1930s, these ballads were being sung throughout the region. All of them used racially charged language to describe Kincaid's death and the pursuit and killing of Miller.

Mellinger Henry, a folk song collector, included "Gladys Kincaid" in his 1934 publication Songs Sung in the Southern Appalachians.

The Montford Murders

On Saturday, June 25, 1927, four days into the Miller manhunt, a story ran in the News & Observer with an intriguing headline: "Wrong Man may be Serving Time." The subhead read, "Possibility that Morganton Negro Committed Crime Laid to Alvin Mansel."

The reporter points out that the 1925 Asheville assault and the Gladys Kincaid murder share similarities. The woman selling flowers on Sunset Mountain said she was struck on the head with a rock and raped. There are also differences: neither Essie Walker nor Gladys Kincaid was raped. Walker was shot and beaten with a bat. Kincaid was bludgeoned to death with a pipe.

Miller, who was 21 at the time of the assault, was also a better match for the woman's description of a tall, light-skinned Black man in his thirties than 17-year-old Mansel. This fact is hardly definitive. All we can really say is that it's clear that Mansel did not commit the crime. Also, we don't know one way or another if Miller was in Asheville in the fall of 1925.

This chain of events brings us to the Montford murders. Two unsolved murders appear to have happened during Miller's time in Asheville. On the night of January 20, 1926, Annie May Burgess, a 23-year-old white woman, was struck on the head with a blunt instrument and killed. A four-foot length of bloodstained metal pipe, although some reports say she was killed with a bottle, was found near the body in a clump of bushes near the intersection of Montford Avenue and Santee Street the next day.

The police arrested three people in connection with the killing. William Davis Burgess' former boyfriend, Caleb Ingram, who reported seeing blood on the sidewalk at the crime scene on the night of the murder, and Bonnie Ledford, who found Burgess' body the next day, There wasn't enough evidence to try any of them for the crime.

On the morning of May 10, 1927, a maid walking to work discovered the body of Mary Cooper, a 61-year-old white woman, in a vacant lot next to her home on Montford Avenue. Cooper had two skull fractures, and her throat was slashed. At first, the police were unaware of the fractures and ruled her death a suicide. A two-foot-long piece of iron pipe was found near her body.

Anna Montague, Cooper's nurse, was charged with the murder and convicted; however, the North Carolina Supreme Court overturned the conviction, stating that there wasn't sufficient evidence. The case remains unsolved.

We don't have hard and fast dates for Miller's time in Asheville, but it looks like he could have been present when Burgess was killed and would have been in town when Cooper was slain.

Could Miller have been a reasonable suspect in the Montford Avenue killings? It's an idea worthy of further research and investigation.

10. The Great West Virginia Train Robbery

Locomotive and log train circa 1915 (Wikimedia Commons: Public Domain).

"Some people steal to stay alive, and some steal to feel alive. Simple as that." — V.E. Schwab, American writer, and novelist, from A Darker Shade of Magic.

About 2 a.m. On October 8, 1915, Train No. 1 of the Baltimore and Ohio Railroad (B&O) had just finished taking on water near Central Station, WV, about 90 miles southeast of Wheeling. No one on the train was aware of the two armed men lurking in the woods behind the water tank.

After the train was underway, engineer Grant Helms looked over his shoulder and saw two masked men climbing over the coal in the tender. Once they were in the locomotive's cab, the men trained their revolvers on Helms and his fireman, C. R. Knight. The taller of the two men instructed the engineer to stop the train at Rock Cut about a half mile down the track.

Once the train was stopped, a third masked man appeared and knocked on the door of the mail car. One of the three mail clerks opened the door, thinking it was a member of the train crew. The man showed the clerk his ticket in the form of a large Colt revolver and was allowed to enter the car. He asked for the head clerk. Haines Huff, the chief clerk, identified himself.

The masked man ordered the other two clerks to leave the car and go to the passenger coaches. He also told them to grab their coats and vests, which they had forgotten in the excitement.

> *"He kept me in the car for a while," Huff told the Fairmont West Virginian. "Then, the bandits cut off the mail car and the locomotive and ran it down the track a way."*

The bandit required Huff to assist him in sorting through the packages. Benjamin Franklin's adage, time is money, was never more appropriate. He tore open some of the envelopes, found they contained money, and threw a number of them into a sack. He would take 90 registered packages of unsigned national bank notes in all.

The bandits made one more stop and released the engineer, fireman, and chief mail clerk. They then rode off with the locomotive, tender, and mail car. Evidently, one of them knew how to operate a locomotive.

They abandoned the train near Duckworth, allowing it to coast down the grade without steam. It rolled to a stop near the Toll Gate water station. The three masked men vanished into the West Virginia woods with more than $100,000 (about $3.2 million today) in unsigned bank notes. Unwittingly, they left behind more than $1 million in cash.

Early the next morning, mere hours after the robbery, U.S. Marshal C. E. Smith and a heavily armed posse with several bloodhounds took up the trail. They chased the bandits over the mountains and through the ravines for three days and nights.

According to an article in the Monday, October 02, 1916 Sheboygan Press:

> *"At one time, the posse was within one mile of the well-hidden camp of the bandits, deep in a ravine, but the dogs became confused at this point and failed to follow the scent."*

But while the hounds couldn't find a trail, the postal inspectors would.

An Interstate Gang of Train Robbers

National banks in the United States could issue banknotes or bills between 1863 and 1935. The U.S. Mint would print the notes and send them to the bank. Before use, each banknote had to be signed by the president of the bank and the head cashier.

The unsigned banknotes left the bandits with two problems. First, they had to fake the signatures on all the banknotes. Second, these banknotes were from the National Bank in Boonville, IN, and the government had a record of the serial numbers. The money was traceable, and spending it would draw attention.

From the April 08, 1917, Washington Post:

> *"The first definite clew was obtained on January 18, 1916, when a stenographer employed by a machinery company at San Antonio, Tex., presented one of the bills for deposit in her postal saving account, bearing the robber-stamped signatures of the officers of a Boonville, Ind., bank, for which it was issued."*

Post Office Inspector Charles G. Kinzel surveyed San Antonio print shops until he found the maker of the rubber stamps. Once Kinzel ran him to ground, the man reluctantly furnished a description of the purchaser and his address.

The stamps had been made for Charles Jefferson "Jeff" Harrison, a blacksmith and mechanic who operated a machine shop and garage in San Antonio. A search of his business turned up a pint fruit jar with $1,755 of the stolen banknotes buried under his garage, the rubber stamps, and what one newspaper described as a "robber's outfit." The 51-year-old Harrison was arrested on January 22, 1916. Subsequent searches found a total of $28,000 in stolen banknotes, both signed and unsigned.

Harrison had a bit of a history with train robbery. In fact, he had been sentenced to life in prison for robbing an East Tennessee, Virginia, and Georgia train near Piedmont, AL, in 1893. That same year, he received a second life sentence for a stagecoach robbery, one account says mail-rider, in Marshall County, AL.

One of his convictions was overturned by the U.S. Supreme Court on appeal in 1896. He was released from the remaining conviction by a pardon from President William McKinley in 1900, secured by a petition drive and his sister, Bertha E. Andrews, traveling to Washington and getting an audience with the president to plead his case.

Harrison paid for both the lawyer's fees and the petition drive by making crafts from seashells in his free time after his prison work hours and selling them to hundreds of people. An article in the Arlington, KS, Enterprise tells us he purchased "fancy shells from the markets of Japan and other remote places."

A Master Train Bandit

Further investigations by postal inspectors and his later confessions would mark him as one of the most prolific train robbers in U.S. history.

The gang was believed to have participated in as many as a dozen train robberies, including:

- Southern Railway robbery, Stevenson, AL., September 1912, $150 taken.

- Illinois Central robbery, Batesville, MS, July 1913, $1,400 taken.

- Alabama Great Southern robbery, Bibbville, AL., September 1913; $2,500 taken.

- Alabama Great Southern robbery Irondale, AL., February 1914; $40,000 in unsigned currency taken.

- Louisville and Nashville robbery, Greenville, AL., July 1915; $500.

After Harrison's arrest, the puzzle pieces came together quickly, and investigators began searching for the other two masked bandits. W. Eugene Diez, 24, of Little Rock, AR, was the man who held the engineer and fireman at bay alongside Harrison. H. Grady Webb (Full name: Henry Grady Webb), 33, of Birmingham, AL., was the man who entered the mail car at Rock Cut and searched in vain for the $1 million in cash that would have set the bandits up for life.

Webb operated a machine shop, an automobile supply store, and a real estate office. Diez was a former Western Union telegraph messenger who had become a plumber.

Sensing that postal inspectors were closing in on him, Webb disappeared from Birmingham on March 30. He was a respected businessman and active in the city's social scene. Newspapers referred to him as "the clubman of Birmingham." His postal service circular showed him in white tie and black dinner jacket with a carnation on his lapel. He proved to be a slippery and determined fugitive.

The Secret Service caught up with Diez at the YMCA in Denver on May 12. Some of the stolen banknotes were found on his person. He later confessed to the robbery and led inspectors to a rocky slope where he had a buried cache containing $16,000 near his home in Hot Springs.

Jeff Harrison's trial began on September 12, 1916, in Martinsburg, WV. He initially pleaded not guilty but sensing that the evidence was overwhelming on the second day of the trial, he stood up and told Judge Alston G. Dayton that he would prefer to change his plea to guilty on seven of the nine counts against him. District Attorney Stuart Walker was happy to oblige, and Harrison was sentenced to 12 years in the Atlanta penitentiary.

The Crime in Detail

Detailed confessions by Harrison and Diez mapped out the crime in full. After years of robbing trains (nearly a quarter century for Harrison), Webb proposed that the gang move its operations closer to Washington, D.C. They wanted to intercept a bulk shipment of cash before it reached Cincinnati and was broken up into many smaller packets. Harrison, who was getting a little too old for the rigors of robberies and the privations of running and hiding that came after them, hoped to make one big final score and retire.

Webb bankrolled the project and was in charge of strategic planning for the robbery. Harrison took tactical charge of the robbery itself. Not only was he the most experienced member of the gang, but he had worked for the railroad in the past and knew how to operate the locomotive. The Sheboygan Press described Diez as the "strong-arm" man of the trio.

Webb traveled to West Virginia a month before the robbery to scout the area, determine the best train to rob and select the time and place for the heist. His observations and calculations led him to choose the B&O No. 1 at the tank stop near Central Station, and he sent for Harrison and Diez.

The only real deviation from Webb's plan was that he originally planned to rob the No. 1 on October 7, but there was a wreck on the rail line, so the gang waited an additional day to strike.

After abandoning the locomotive at Duckworth, the gang headed north, hiking through the woods. At daylight, they hid in the timber on a high ridge. When night fell, they struck out to the west. After three nights of travel, they reached St Marys on the Ohio River. There, they divided the loot and caught trains to their respective designations: San Antonio, Birmingham, and Hot Springs.

From Ringleader to Fugitive

That left postal inspectors and Secret Service agents with the small task of finding, arresting, trying, and incarcerating H. Grady Webb. They offered a $1,000 reward, printed circulars with his photo and physical particulars, and searched nationwide. In December 1916, they apprehended a traveling salesman in Alexandria, VA, who fit Webb's description and transported him all the way to Martinsburg, only to have Diez tell them they had the wrong man.

From the April 04, 1917, Montgomery Advertiser:

> *"The chase for Webb, which began at Birmingham, Ala., in March 1916, and ended in Kansas City, Mo., last January, was as pretty a man hunt as the government ever engaged in, and when the story was told it equaled anything in the whole range of detective literature."*

In January 1917, James C. Wright, a student at the Eclectic Medical University in Kansas City, MO., noticed that one of his first-year classmates, Wallace White, looked oddly familiar. Realizing that he had recognized White from a wanted poster, Wright was able to confirm his identification of White as Webb because of a ridge on his left thumbnail, which had been described on the poster. He contacted postal inspectors.

Inspector J. M. Donaldson, accompanied by two city detectives, arrested Webb on January 16, removing him from one of the university's classrooms.

Webb and Diez had their day of reckoning on April 3, 1917, at the Martinsburg courthouse. Webb pleaded guilty on all nine counts, and District Attorney Walker noted that the maximum sentence allowable was 75 years, but he would be satisfied with 25. Webb was not only the ringleader, but he also endangered the lives of the three mail clerks when he entered the mail car with a drawn revolver. Diez received a 10-year sentence due to his cooperation and his youth.

The next day, in route to prison in Atlanta, Webb escaped custody in Charlotte, N.C. While the train was stopped at the station, he leaped through a window and dashed off into the night. He was recaptured on April 12 in Badin, N.C., near Salisbury, about 50 miles from Charlotte. The police found him working in the plumbing department of the aluminum plant there. An article in the Charlotte Observer said, "He took the arrest philosophically, admitting that he was the man wanted."

There was another bright note to the West Virginia robbery because Harrison confessed to the Central Station robbery and several other robberies, including one in Bibbville, AL. Three men, Harry Marks, Frank Moore, and Frank Williams, who had been convicted of the Bibbville heist and were serving 25-year prison terms, were pardoned by President Woodrow Wilson on Sunday, August 12, 1917.

Epilogue

Eugene Diez disappeared from the newspapers, which probably means he decided to pursue his trade as a plumber, avoiding posses, trials, and prison cells.

The last mention we could find of Grady Webb was an item about him editing a monthly magazine called "Good Words" in the Atlanta Penitentiary in 1921. It described him as a model prisoner.

Jeff Harrison was paroled in 1925. While working in the prison's duck (canvas) mill, he invented and later patented an automatic loom stop device (J. Harrison: Automatic knock-off and hook-stop for looms (1,615,082) issued January 18, 1927). According to an Associated Press (AP) article, the device was a commercial success.

11. A Deadly Reunion at Runion

Postcard of the Carolina Special Circa 1913. (UNC Library: Public Domain).

"The justifications of men who kill should always be heard with skepticism, said the monster." A Monster Calls — Patrick Ness, British-American author, journalist, lecturer, and screenwriter.

It was almost like a Sherlock Holmes story. A body was discovered, and foul play was suspected. A postmortem examination gave the cause of death as strangulation. The nearby crime scene showed signs of a struggle, as well as footprints belonging to the victim, the killer, and a supposed confederate, and the tracks of a horse or mule leading away. Bloodhounds were summoned. Clandestine railway travel was uncovered. Unfortunately, this story set in the mill village of Runion, N.C., in 1920, was all too real and all too tragic.

At about 10:15 p.m. on Monday, August 23, 1920, 33-year-old Frank Henderson got off the Southern Railroad No. 27 train, the Carolina

Special, at Barnard and started toward home on foot. A waxing gibbous moon lit his way. Curiously, he did not get off the train at Sandy Bottom or Runion, which would have put him closer to his destination. According to his draft card filled out three years earlier, Henderson was a tall man of medium build with blue eyes and light hair. His occupation was listed as self-employed farmer.

It had been some time since he had been home to see his wife, Ella, and their five children, whose ages ranged from five months to 10 years old. Neighbors testified that he had been absent for three to five months. He had been living in Spartanburg, S.C., and was seen multiple times in the company of 20-year-old Gertrude Sams, who court records called his confederate and newspapers referred to as his sweetheart.

As he continued on his way to Sandy Bottom, about a mile from Betsy's Siding, he came upon a man with whiskey, who Henderson said gave him two or three drinks, which may have made him drunk. When Henderson got to his family's home, he saw a man talking with his wife on the porch and a mule tied nearby. He decided to continue walking down the road a short distance and sat down. The man got on the mule and left. Ella came down to where he was, and they began to talk.

An argument broke out, with each of them accusing the other of infidelity. The conflict became physical, and he choked her. He claimed that she recovered, and they walked back to the house, where she sat on the porch and he sat in the yard. After a few minutes, she fell over. He thought she was crying and went up to her and saw that she was dead. This realization sobered him up, and he "straightened her out" and left. He went back down the road to Betsy's Siding, passing there about three o'clock in the morning, and jumped aboard a passing freight train at Rollins' and rode it into Asheville. From there, he took the early morning train to Spartanburg.

This was Frank Henderson's explanation of the events of the night of his wife's death. However, physical evidence from the crime scene and witness statements quickly sent the story in another, more sinister direction.

On the morning of August 24, 1920, at about 6:30, the body of Mary Lou "Ella" Henderson was found by her children on their porch. One of the children, most likely Pauline, the oldest, called out to the first person who passed by Mack Waterberger, who summoned nearby neighbors, Mrs. Bonnie Norton and Mrs. Rector. They were soon joined by others from the community as word spread.

Ella Henderson was found lying on her back, barefoot, and wearing her night clothes. There were fragments of grass and leaves in her hair. According to newspaper reports, she had heard a noise on the front porch the night before and went out to investigate. A few articles say one of the children heard a man knock on the front door and call out "mama" multiple times. Ella did not return and was not seen again alive.

When Deputy Sheriff Matthew Ramsey arrived at about 8:00 a.m., he found the Henderson's neighbors guarding the body on the porch and a place across the road where tracks, disturbed ground, and upturned leaves indicated a struggle had taken place.

Near the porch, they found tracks made by two people wearing shoes. Several witnesses described these at trial. The tracks were presumed to be that of a man and a woman based on size and the deeper heel impressions of the smaller tracks. There were also barefoot tracks believed to belong to Ella, which only pointed away from the house. About 77 steps from the small wooden cabin in a level spot above the road covered with old dead leaves, searchers found "a confused mass of footprints that indicated a struggle." Here, searchers found a hairpin that matched the other hairpins in the deceased's hair.

About 75 yards past the house on the road to Walnut, Deputy Sheriff Ramsey saw what he described in testimony as tracks left by the heels of a woman's shoes about three feet up on a bank near some mule tracks in the road. It looked to him like a woman had climbed the bank to mount the mule.

Sometime between 5:00 and 5:30 pm, Madison County Sheriff Jesse James Bailey and the Coroner, Dr. J. N. Moore, arrived. Shortly after, the sheriff and the doctor, John A. Lyerly, Captain of the Asheville Police Department, arrived with his well-known bloodhounds. Bailey had sent for him and the dogs upon hearing of the crime. A 1922 article in the Raleigh News and Observer describes Lyerly and his lead bloodhound, Joe the Fourth, as veterans of more than 300 manhunts.

All these men, the policemen, the doctor, and the bloodhound tracking specialist, traveled to and from the crime scene by train. In a 1978 interview, Bailey stated that during his term as Madison County Sheriff, there were only five cars and two taxis in the entire county.

Dr. Moore held the postmortem examination of the deceased's body that day. He found a frothy mucus issuing from the mouth and nose, imprints of fingernails on each side of her throat, black and blue spots on her left arm and right leg. This discoloration extended over the lower part of her throat and the back of it and over almost her entire back, as well as parts of both arms and legs. He further stated that, in his opinion, she died of strangulation.

In other words, Ella Henderson had been severely beaten and choked to death.

Behind the Hounds

Lyerly and the hounds were taken to where the struggle took place, and the dogs, Joe and Nell, set to work, leading first to the porch where Ella's body lay, then up the road toward Walnut.

The tracking party was made up of the dogs, followed by Lyerly, followed by three Madison County Deputies: Caton, Ramsey, and Treadway, followed by a crowd of about 30 people.

Imagine if you lived in this community and happened to look out a window and see this procession passing by. Would you say to yourself: "Well, there's something you don't see every day," or would you grab your hat and a lantern and take out after them?

In about 100 yards, they lost the scent but picked it up again when they found a mule's track in the road that led them a half mile further. They came to a road on the right that branched off the main road. It was here that "dark overtook us." The road led to a path, which led to a yard, which led to the house of John and Mary Chandler, Frank Henderson's sister, in an area known as Hickory Flats, about five miles from the Henderson house. And sitting on the porch with them was one Gertrude Sams.

> "The old dog put his feet up on the porch, and the other dog came to the old dog, and they both stopped," said Lyerly. "The Sams woman was sitting there. He (old Joe) was closest to the Sams woman."

The 1920 Census shows Gertrude Sams and her 5-year-old son, Claude, and 3-year-old daughter, Melissa, living with Gertrude's grandfather, Leat Norton, in the Big Laurel community about 15 miles from Hickory Flats as the crow flies. The census record does not mention her husband, Grant Sams, living there.

In her trial testimony, Mary stated that Gertrude had come to the Chandler house about 6:00 pm on Saturday, two days before the murder, and she had invited Gertrude and her daughter to stay the night. Mary also testified that Gertrude had mentioned seeing Frank Henderson in Asheville that Saturday. She didn't give much in the way of explanation about why Gertrude and the girl were still there on Tuesday night. Both John and Mary testified that Gertrude was there when they went to bed Monday night and when they got up Tuesday morning. Mary further stated that she had only seen her once before, when Gertrude and Frank stopped by her house just for a minute or two at 10:00 one night. The deputies took Sams into custody and transported her to Marshall.

Frank Henderson was arrested by Madison County Deputies in Marshall "when he alighted from an Asheville train," as one newspaper put it, on the same day that his wife's body was found. He claimed that he had been in Spartanburg for the last week and was unaware of his wife's death; at least, that was the first story he told.

Henderson and Sams were transferred to the Buncombe County jail for safekeeping by Sheriff Bailey and were held there pending trial at the next criminal term of the Superior court in Madison County. As one paper put it, this was "Owing to the intense feeling which officers say exists in that county."

On August 29, Sheriff Bailey questioned Henderson in the Buncombe County jail in the presence of Sheriff Mitchell and other witnesses. Henderson confessed to choking his wife and exonerated Gertrude Sams. The details of his confession were the basis for our introduction.

From the Monday, August 30, Asheville Citizen:

> *"The Sams woman was not with me, and we did not make our escape on the mule," Henderson said. "The other man got away on the mule, I believe since I remember seeing it tied near a rock when I approached the house."*

There were glaring holes in Henderson's confession. The man Henderson claimed he saw talking with his wife on the porch was never found. He also gave no explanation for the small footprints that appeared to belong to a woman wearing shoes, the leaves and grass in Ella Henderson's hair, or the bruises on her back, arms, and legs. He did not mention the signs of a struggle or the hairpin found nearly 100 yards away from the cabin and yard, where he said the argument occurred.

The state contended that there was evidence of a motive to "put the wife out of the way." The defendant had deserted his wife and children, according to the evidence, and had gone to another state and was living in adultery with his codefendant, Gertrude Sams. Further, the court asserted that he was intent on selling the home where his wife and children lived, but Ella Henderson refused to join in the execution of the deed.

On Wednesday, September 28, Henderson and Sams were tried as codefendants in Superior Court for first-degree murder. The defense maintained that Henderson's confession did not prove murder in the first degree and that there was no premeditation. In short, he did not plan or intend to kill his wife. It just happened. Basically, they argued for manslaughter, which was the best they could hope for, given Henderson's confession.

Whether Henderson was guilty of manslaughter or first-degree murder hinged on premeditation. The prosecution contended that on the afternoon of the homicide, Henderson, in his travels from Spartanburg to Barnard, tried to conceal himself from other passengers on the train who might recognize him.

Will Holt, a Southern Railway worker, saw Henderson on the train the night of the murder and again the next evening when Henderson came back to Marshall, where he was arrested.

> *"He was standing between the cars in the vestibule,"*
> *Holt said. "He had on a black coat, and a pair of*
> *overalls, and a black hat, with his hat, pulled down on*
> *the right side, looking kinder towards the river – head*
> *down towards the river."*

Holt had known Henderson for more than a decade and attempted to engage him in conversation, but Henderson avoided him. When Holt saw him the following evening, he noticed some rather telling changes in Henderson's appearance.

> *"The next night, he was clean-shaved had on a*
> *different hat and better clothes. I noticed a few*

scratches on his jaw, a little more on the left than on the right side. ... It looked like somebody might have pulled a little hunk out of his jaw."

On Friday night, Judge Ben F. Long charged the jury, and 12 hours later, they rendered their verdict, finding Henderson guilty of murder in the first degree. Judge Long sentenced him to be electrocuted at Central Prison in Raleigh on November 12. Henderson's defense team immediately filed an appeal.

On December 24, the N.C. Supreme Court found no error and upheld the conviction. The ruling has been cited multiple times in murder cases due to its findings regarding premeditation. The following is a brief summary.

"We think upon this evidence, the jury may well have inferred that the killing of the wife by the husband was premeditated and deliberate. It doesn't require any great length of time to elapse between the time when the design to kill is formed and when it is put into execution. When the purpose of killing is weighed long enough to form a fixed design to kill, and at a subsequent time, no matter how soon or how remote, it is put into execution, there is sufficient premonition and deliberation to constitute murder in the first degree."

On September 15, Governor Cameron A. Morrison reviewed Henderson's case and declined the request to commute his sentence to life in prison. The next day, a headline on page nine of the Charlotte Observer read: No Pardon for Wife Murderer. With stays and appeals, Frank Henderson's appointment with the electric chair moved to October 10, 1921.

Gertrude Sams was found not guilty. Really, the jury had no choice. Judge Long had instructed them that "Evidence that bloodhounds trailed a human being is never sufficient by itself and unsupported to sustain a conviction."

Gertrude insisted that she had not been present when Ella Henderson was killed. Frank Henderson swore that Gertrude was not present. And the only other potential witness, Ella Henderson, could not testify.

The Chair of Chained Lightning

When Dr. W. McC. White, pastor of the First Presbyterian Church, Raleigh, N.C., called on Frank Henderson at 10:00 on October 10, 1921, a half hour before the condemned man was scheduled to be electrocuted, he handed the reverend an 8-10 page letter. The handwritten document was described by Henderson as a "true statement, unjust sentence."

One of Henderson's fellow inmates had taught him to read and write during his year of incarceration. He told the reverend that he had been working on the statement for several days and asked him to give it to the press after his execution.

At the appointed time, accompanied by Reverend White, Henderson walked the 100 feet from his cell to the death room. Pausing at the doorway, he shook hands with Warden Sam J. Busbee and is reported to have said, "Goodbye, Mr. Busbee," he said. "I don't hold anything against you."

Multiple newspaper accounts say that Henderson wept or sobbed during the walk to the room and broke and cried getting into the chair. All accounts agree that he sat in the chair unassisted and was silent while the attendants strapped him in. The Raleigh News & Observer mentions 33 spectators grouped in a semicircle around the chair. According to the paper's account:

> *"The body snapped tight under the force of the current (1,800 volts) that surged through it. The neck muscles bulged. The right hand clenched. For 30 seconds, the*

*current had its play, and then the body dropped back
in the chair limp. The warden pulled the switch twice
more, and the electric power coursed through
Henderson's frame with the same reaction."*

Dr. Norwood, the prison physician, checked the body for vital signs;
there were none. He pronounced Frank Henderson dead, making him the
third of seven prisoners executed in 1921 and the 52nd person to die in
the state's electric chair.

True Statement: Unjust Sentence

Henderson's final written confession was, for the most part, the same as
the one he gave to the two sheriffs and other witnesses in the Buncombe
County jail. There were a few notable additions. At one point, he said
that when his wife became unresponsive, he went to get a doctor and that
hopping a freight train was part of that task, but he passed out drunk and
did not wake until a railroad worker roused him in the train yard in
Asheville. He also said that his wife had a goiter and a heart condition,
which caused her to die. Henderson's handwritten final confession was
difficult to understand in places, and newspapers cleaned up the spelling
and punctuation as best they could.

> *"I know it was not in my heart to do what I did, and it
> could not of been abusement caused death of wife. If
> hadn't been, the condition of her health would not
> have been but a fuss fight of it all,"* Henderson wrote.

The News and Observer also ran a statement from O.B. Burnett,
presumably a physician, who claimed to have treated Ella Henderson for
goiter and stated that it could have been the cause of death. Burnett also
described Frank Henderson as a man of good character and "in my
estimation and numbers of others he didn't have a fair trial."

In summary, Henderson beat his wife, choked her to death, left her body
on the front porch for his children to find the next morning, and in his

final written statement, blamed her death on her ill health, which he knew about before he assaulted her. Even those who oppose the death penalty on moral grounds might have been willing to make an exception in his case.

Epilogue

The village of Runion is a ghost town today. All that is left of a once thriving community of 1,200 people is a few scattered ruins. The lumber mill closed in 1925. You can see its brick chimneys and crumbling foundations from the Laurel River Trail. Parking for the 3.6-mile hiking path can be found at the intersection of SR 208 and US 25/US 70.

The trail follows the old railroad bed that was used to carry logs to the Runion sawmill in the 1920s. The grade is mild, with an elevation change of 220 feet from the trailhead to the French Broad River. There are a couple of spots along the path where rocks and roots make trail shoes or hiking boots a good choice. The views of the scenic gorge and towering bluffs are worth your time.

Orphaned by the murder of their mother and the execution of their father, the Henderson children were split up and sent to live with relatives.

The 1930 Census shows Margaret Henderson and Mary Hester Henderson living with George and Nita Gentry in Rock Hill, S.C. At some point they returned to Madison County and died within two months of each other that same year. Margaret was 12 and a student. She died of double pneumonia. Mary was 17 and a textile worker. She succumbed to myocarditis and aortic and mitral insufficiency.

The 1930 Census shows Pauline married to Hezekiah Chandler, living in Marshall with a newborn daughter. We could not find where John was living that year, but he would have been 16. Guy, who changed his name to Frank Jr., was living in Asheville with his uncle and aunt. The remaining three Henderson children lived long, full lives. Frank Jr. was 82 when he died. Pauline and John lived into their 90s.

Mary Hester Henderson (15 Nov 1912 – 23 Sep 1930) Stackhouse Cemetery, Stackhouse, N.C.

Margaret Henderson (15 Nov 1918 – 24 Nov 1930) Stackhouse Cemetery, Stackhouse, N.C.

Frank Henderson Jr. (25 Mar 1920 – 23 June 2002) Forest Hills Cemetery, Rock Hill, S.C.

Pauline Elizabeth Henderson Chandler (13 Apr 1910 – 29 Sep 2003) Hillcrest Memorial Gardens Cemetery, Dandridge, TN

John Edward Henderson (12 Sep 1914 – 8 Mar 2011) Fort Jackson National Cemetery, Columbia, S. C.

Frank Henderson was buried in the Henderson Cemetery (Hickory Flats) Walnut, N.C., no stone marks the grave. We could not discover where Ella Henderson was buried.

Gertrude Sams married Branson Chandler in 1924. She died in 1939 at the age of 39. Her death certificate gives the cause of death as "No doctor, cause of death supposed to be from internal cancer." It notes that she was buried in the Revere Cemetery.

(Editor's Note Regarding Names)

Some of the names in this chapter are problematic and confusing.

Ella Henderson's full name was Mary Lou Ella Southerland Henderson. The Henderson's marriage license and the birth certificate of their youngest child, Guy Henderson, record her unmarried name as Ella Southerland. Most newspaper articles refer to her as Mrs. Frank Henderson or Mrs. Henderson. A few reports do reference her as Mary L. Henderson.

Frank Henderson's full name was James William Franklin Henderson. All the documents we found gave his name as Frank Henderson.

Gertrude Sams is referred to as Gertrude Sams in court documents and most newspaper accounts, but some reports gave her name as Susie Sams.

Finally, Guy Henderson, the youngest of the Henderson children, at some point changed his name to Frank Henderson Jr.

12. The Old Money Murder

Knoxville Skyline from Postcard Circa 1930-1945 (Wikimedia Commons: Public Domain).

"A miser grows rich by seeming poor. An extravagant man grows poor by seeming rich," — *William Shenstone, English poet, amateur landscape gardener, and collector.*

On Sunday, March 12, 1939, around noontime, 72-year-old Harriet Beasley went to check on her brother, 62-year-old William "Willie" D. Ledford, at his home in Spring Creek, NC. She was accompanied by Celia Fleming, the wife of one of Ledford's tenants.

They found the kitchen door open, the house ransacked, belongings and money scattered on the floor, a pool of blood in the kitchen, and a trail of blood stains leading from there to the bedroom. On the bedroom floor lay Willie Ledford, bound hand and foot and covered by bedclothes and random items. A towel had been stuffed in his mouth as a gag.

Ledford's head had multiple deep lacerations. His nose was crushed, and his face was a collection of bruises and cuts. Two skull fractures had caused his death.

Beasley went to a neighbor's house about a half mile away to use his phone to report the crime. Thus began the investigation into one of the most brutal and bizarre crimes that Madison County Sheriff Guy English would encounter in his career.

According to the Monday, March 13, Asheville Citizen, Ledford's hands, legs, and feet had been bound with cheesecloth, and only his feet were visible from under the bedclothes. Three bloodstained "pieces of lumber" were found near the body. Robbery was believed to have been the motive for the murder. From the article:

> *"Sheriff English said that he believed that Mr. Ledford recognized his attackers and that they killed him before robbing him of an undetermined amount of money. It was generally believed that Mr. Ledford kept a large sum of money in his house. The money, officers were told, was in large-sized bills which are no longer in general circulation."*

Ledford was a wealthy recluse known to keep a good bit of cash around his house. He was also rumored to have recently made a large timber sale worth $3,500.

There is an old Appalachian saying that goes something like, "That old codger has every nickel that he ever earned." While this colorful expression is unlikely to ever be entirely true, Willie Ledford came close to this accomplishment.

As noted by the Asheville Citizen and the Morristown, TN, Gazette Mail the day after the murder, some of the money Ledford had stored away, both bills and coins, was decades old. In some cases, the money's age was easy to spot because many of the bills were larger, and many of the silver coins were tarnished with age. Ten years earlier, in 1929, the size of US banknotes changed. The government had made the bills about 30 percent smaller to lower printing costs.

> "Ledford was a quiet and frugal man and never told anyone of his financial status," said Sheriff English. "From what relatives and friends have told us. However, we believe there may have been as much as $10,000 (about $221,400 today) in the house when he was slain."

"An Erroneous Exchange of Hats"

The crime scene was littered with evidence, but a few oddities stood out.

A week earlier, on Sunday, March 5, while Ledford was away from home, someone had broken into his house and stolen $130, mostly in one-dollar bills. In both the burglary and the murder, entry was made through the kitchen window. English didn't think this was a coincidence. Also, whoever climbed through the window left strands of red hair on the sash.

While the red hairs could not be definitively traced to an individual, forensic DNA testing didn't come along until 1986; the hair significantly narrowed the field. Red or "ginger" hair is found in two to six percent of people of northern European ancestry and even less in other populations.

Investigators found a hat. There was one catch, though no one they showed the hat to could recall ever seeing Ledford wear it. If the hat didn't belong to the victim, whose hat was it? In their haste to depart the crime scene in the half-light of early morning, one of the culprits had mistakenly taken Ledford's hat and left his own. English later told the Johnson City Chronicle that this clue helped him solve the case.

An old heavy trunk had been broken into. Later, it was discovered that the trunk was the source of the items thrown on top of Ledford's body, the bills scattered on the floor, and the four handkerchiefs found near Ledford's body. These had been used to hold money. One of the handkerchiefs still had a small amount of change tied in one corner.

Enter Mr. Davis and Mr. Plemmons

On Tuesday, March 14, two Knox County Deputies, Bruce Newman and M. H. Underwood, arrested Frank Davis of Monroe, N.C., and Willard Plemmons of Cosby, TN, at a roadhouse called the Moonlight Garden just outside Knoxville. Plemmons had red hair. The two young men said they met in Charlotte and were headed to Cincinnati.

The roadhouse proprietor, Raymond Meredith, had called the Knox County Sheriff's Office due to his growing suspicion of the men, which was prompted by the fact that some of the money they used to buy beer "appeared to be old and tarnished."

When the men were booked in the Knox County jail, officers discovered they had $1,574.53 in cash on them (about $34,864.97 today's money). The money found on the suspects included a $10 gold piece and $10 in silver. These coins had dates ranging from 1890 to 1907, according to a report in the March 16 Asheville Citizen.

Knox County Sheriff Carroll Cate called Sheriff English and asked him to come take a look at the suspects. It turns out that English knew the two men and had, in fact, been looking for them. He identified Willard Plemmons as Edward B. Duckett, 21, and Frank Davis as William Doyle Duckett, 20. The men were both from Spring Creek and first cousins. One wonders if Sheriff English gave Edward his hat back. The sheriff took them to Marshall, N.C., and then moved them to the Buncombe County jail in Asheville for safekeeping.

An Early Morning Ambush

The Duckett cousins had left Waynesville Saturday morning and arrived at Ledford's home between 7:00 and 8:00 a.m. Sunday morning. They waited until the old man got up and went to milk his cows. When they saw him heading for the barn, Edward Duckett climbed through a window and opened the kitchen door for Doyle. In his haste to get into the house, Edward scraped his head on the window sash, leaving behind the telltale hairs found by investigators. Picking up sticks of kindling in the kitchen, they waited to ambush the old man.

Ledford walked into the house, and the young men clubbed him with the sticks. The first couple of blows didn't knock him down, so they clubbed him again. He hit the floor groaning, and they tied his hands and feet and carried him to the bedroom. The cousins took money from Ledford's person and used a hammer to break open a trunk, where they found quite a pile of cash. They quickly ransacked the rest of the house and left.

The day of the murder was not the Ducketts' first visit to the Ledford residence. A week earlier, on Sunday, March 5, while Ledford was away from home, the cousins broke into his house and stole $130.

They headed to Waynesville, about 30 miles south of Spring Creek in Haywood County, where they spent several days. There, the young men made themselves conspicuous by going on a spending spree.

They mostly stayed with their friend Viney Lanning but spent a night at Bob Gaddy's house and gave his children two gold watches, a man's wristwatch, and a woman's pocket watch. The watches didn't work, so the Gaddys took them to a local jeweler who noticed that the name Laura Ledford was engraved on the case of the pocket watch. She was Willie Ledford's younger sister, who had passed away in 1919.

According to the March 16, 1939, Waynesville Mountaineer, many of the dollar bills the Ducketts were spending were from the larger-size 1923 series, which caught people's attention. Deputy Sheriff Noble Ferguson secured 16 of the bills from local stores in what appears to have been the beginning of an investigation by the Haywood County Sheriff's Department.

At trial, Sheriff English testified that in their confessions, the young men admitted that it was in Waynesville the Friday before the murder that they made their plan to return and rob Ledford.

The Unlucky 13th Juror

On May 24, Doyle and Edward Duckett went on trial for the murder of Willie Ledford. Both plead not guilty by reason of insanity. Defense counsel moved for separate trials for the two youths, but the motion was denied. The state made a strong case and presented multiple witnesses.

Sheriff English testified about the defendants' confessions made while in the Buncombe County jail. The presiding judge, J. A. Rousseau, permitted the written statements to be introduced as evidence. The defense objected, contending the confessions had been obtained under pressure. On the other hand, the state argued that the confessions were obtained after the defendants had been warned that anything they said would be held against them and that they had given the statements of their own free will.

The now-familiar Miranda warning did not become part of U.S. law until the 1966 Miranda v. Arizona US Supreme Court decision.

Edward E. Dunn, who prepared Ledford's body for burial, testified that, in his opinion, the cause of death was two severe skull fractures and went on to describe nine other gashes on the victim's head.

Ledford's sister, Harriet Beasley, testified about finding his body and identified the pocket watch that had her sister's name engraved on it that the Ducketts had given to the Gaddy children.

A.L. Hashe, a railroad detective and fingerprint expert from Morristown, TN, a small city about 60 miles west of Marshall, testified that Doyle Duckett's fingerprints were the same as those found on a window pane at the Ledford home.

Leone Smith, who operated a lodge at Max Patch, said the Duckett boys ate dinner at her place the Monday after the murder and paid for it with an 1898 silver half-dollar.

Dr. W. A. Sams, a Marshall physician, testified that any of Ledford's ten wounds could have caused his death.

The witnesses for the defense were less authoritative and less convincing.

Doyle's sister, Naomi Duckett, testified that insanity ran in the family, saying an uncle, cousin, and other family members had mental difficulties. On cross-examination, she admitted that she had never met any of them and was relying on stories passed down in the family.

J. T. Chappell, who taught Doyle in the seventh grade, testified that the young man had below-average grades but was well-behaved. Romaine Meadows took the stand as a character witness for Doyle.

However, the state's robust case was derailed by a procedural error. Court officials discovered that the 13th, or alternate Juror, had not been dismissed before the jury began deliberations. Defense counsel moved for the mistrial, and Judge J. Will Pless, Jr., had no choice but to allow the motion. According to a May 26 Asheville Citizen article, Sheriff Guy English said afterward that the jury was hopelessly deadlocked, and the case probably would have ended in a mistrial anyway.

An Awfully Bad Verdict

On September 5, the case was brought before the NC Supreme Court, appealing against a second trial for the Ducketts. Defense counsel James M. Bailey argued that a new trial would constitute double jeopardy and contended the judge should have called for a verdict from the 12 qualified jurors. The court dismissed the appeal.

The Ducketts' second trial began on December 1. The people who attended or reported on the two trials described them as carbon copies, with essentially the same evidence, testimony, and arguments. A notable exception was that Edward Duckett took the witness stand on his own behalf in the second trial.

He testified that he and Doyle went to the Ledford home a week before the death, stole $2,200, and hid the money in a stump except for $80. He said they returned to the Ledford's home a week later to get a drink of water.

Edward further stated that after Ledford gave them water, the farmer questioned them about the robbery at his home, became angry, and pulled out a white-handled knife. Edward said he and Doyle picked up sticks of stove wood and struck Ledford because they were afraid he was going to cut them.

Superior Court Judge J. A. Rousseau pointed out that since Duckett had not previously mentioned Ledford threatening the two men with a knife, the jury might disregard his testimony.

Edward and Doyle Duckett were found guilty of second-degree murder and sentenced to 30 years at hard labor under the supervision of the state highway commission. According to the December 2 Asheville Times, before sentencing the defendants, Judge Rousseau stated that:

The verdict was "awfully bad" and said, "The jury could easily have found the two defendants guilty of murder in the first degree under the evidence."

The cousins had narrowly missed a trip to the gas chamber.

Not So Great Escape Artists

The December 1939 trial would not be the Duckett boys' last appearance in the newspapers. Doyle escaped custody twice and Edward three times, but they were recaptured each time.

In September 1940, Edward Duckett jumped from a wagon and dashed across a cornfield in an attempt to escape from the Caledonia state prison farm in Halifax, N.C. Guard J. T. Smith fired once into the air, and when Duckett did not halt, he shot him in the left shoulder.

In September 1942, Doyle Duckett was part of a 10-prisoner escape from the Watauga County Prison Camp near Boone. Two weeks later, he surrendered to officers at Marshall. In 1948, Doyle made a second escape, this time from a Transylvania County prison camp. He made it all the way to Pasadena, TX, before being caught.

In June 1945, Edward Duckett was part of a three-prisoner escape in which Foreman Carl Keith was killed. He and L. D. Hatchell were convicted of second-degree murder and sentenced to an additional 25 years. The third prisoner, J. A. McKeitham, was killed in a shootout with the police near Newbridge in Buncombe County. Duckett was captured at his parent's home in Spring Creek. He was unarmed and offered no resistance.

In April 1950, Edward Duckett and Leroy Newell escaped from a Halifax County road gang and were recaptured the next day.

Epilogue

Both men served the rest of their sentences in the North Carolina prison system without further incidents or headlines. In December 1953, Doyle Duckett was paroled after serving 14 years. In March of 1959, Edward Duckett was also paroled after serving 19 years. The cousins seem to have finally learned that crime doesn't pay or, at least, that the bonus on the front end wasn't worth the payments on the back end.

13. The Dangerous Pastime of Freighthopping

Freight-hopping youths circa 1940. (NARA: Public Domain).

"The thing about plummeting downhill at fifty miles an hour on a snack platter - if you realize it's a bad idea when you're halfway down, it's too late." — *Richard Riordan, American author.*

Five teenage boys were passing through the town of Marshall, N.C., at one o'clock on a Friday morning in the late 1970s. It was a clear, warm night, and a freight train slowly rumbled southward down the tracks between the river and the town's buildings.

One of them commented on the languid pace of the train. Another pointed out that several of the boxcars moving through the railroad crossing appeared to be empty, with the large sliding door on the side of the train car open.

"You know, a couple of us could jump on one of those boxcars and ride to Asheville. We could get off at the rail yard. Someone could follow us in the truck and bring us back."

The late hour, the ages of those involved, and the camaraderie of the group made the determination that this was an excellent idea. The truck driver and a passenger watched as the other three ran, stumbling beside the open door of one of the boxcars.

The loose, large gray granite rocks slid and rolled under their feet until the larger of the three youths successfully scrambled in through one of the open doors and managed to drag each of the two smaller boys in with him.

Having seen their companions make it into the boxcar, the other two boys turned and ran for the parked truck, intent on keeping pace with the train as it headed to Asheville, following what the locals used to call the river road, now known as Old Marshall Highway or NC 251.

Just outside town, the train crossed a steel truss bridge, putting it on the opposite side of the French Broad River from the road as it snaked its way toward Asheville, picking up speed as it went.

The three young men watched the scenery pass by through the boxcar's open door. All three had traveled in the same direction many times. However, this was the first time their observations were made from their current perspective. Seeing the river, houses, and businesses roll by in the dim light was mentally absorbing. The train continued to accelerate until it reached the small town of Woodfin. It slowed for the numerous crossings there.

The boys had long since lost sight of their pursuit truck. The train slowed as it entered Asheville, the boxcar rider's planned destination.

The three were proud of their adventure and achievement. They prepared for the train to slow more in the railyard to dismount the moving boxcar safely. To their surprise, the train began to accelerate. Unfortunately, by the time they confirmed the increase in speed, they were traveling too fast to safely leap from the boxcar to the now swiftly moving ground.

The train continued to accelerate and did not appear to be stopping anytime soon. Between brief flashes of street and security lights, one of the riders' Timex wristwatch showed that an hour and 45 minutes elapsed before the train slowed enough for the now unwilling passengers to disembark.

Leaping from the train, the once fearless adventurers were deposited in an unknown land. Not knowing where they were and seeing flashlights of what they thought were railroad yard security, the three found themselves running to the nearby highway.

Once more, in the light, they tried to come up with a plan to deal with this new, unanticipated dilemma. Sighting a 24-hour gas station, they went inside to determine their whereabouts. The clerk informed the trio they were in Marion, about 55 miles from their starting point in Marshall. The store attendant appeared unsurprised about the boys' predicament, as if such poorly chosen adventures were commonplace there, which, in fact, they were.

Once directed to an outside payphone, with much trial and error, one adventurer's father was enticed to accept the charges of a collect call. Thus, they got a ride home, complete with a constant lecture from the unhappy-to-be-awakened relative. This was not the end of the story, though.

The boys spent the following summer working without compensation at homes, businesses, and farms as a punishment for the misadventure. The preceding tale occurred in 1979. I later learned that variations of this story had occurred numerous times.

Railroad Hazards

This is an excellent point to mention that freight hopping, also known as train hopping, is a dangerous and foolhardy activity. According to Federal Railroad Administration statistics, 1,226 pedestrian rail trespass casualties occurred in 2022, including 555 injuries and 671 fatalities.

Special Agent Joe Talley, a law enforcement officer with Norfolk Southern, described a few of the risks of illegal train riding, including death and dismemberment, getting locked in a boxcar, having the 900-pound door slammed on you, or falling asleep and falling off a moving train, in a 2016 article in the Asheville Mountain Xpress, written by Max Hunt.

> *"You're riding on equipment that wasn't designed to be ridden on. The very nature of the railroad is unforgiving. There are no second chances," Talley said in the article.*

At least one railway accident made medical history. In 1962, 12-year-old Everett Knowles, Jr., attempted to hop a train in Boston. One of the freight train's wheels severed his right arm just below the shoulder. A team of surgeons at Massachusetts General Hospital was able to reattach the arm. This was the first replantation of a severed human limb.

A follow-up article in the Boston Globe in 1971 noted that after five additional operations to rejoin nerves, tendons, muscles, and blood vessels, Knowles regained near-normal sensation and function in the arm. At that time, he was holding down two jobs: mail clerk and night watchman.

In addition to the life-and-limb hazards of train hopping, legal issues can range from simple trespassing to unlawfully riding on the train or even interfering with railroad operations. In North Carolina, the punishments can include substantial fines and several months in jail. You can also face federal charges.

A Well-Worn Path

I spoke with another gentleman who told me almost the same narrative, except his train-hopping experience occurred in 1966. He provided me with the name of one of his cohorts who accompanied him on his trip, whom I was able to contact to confirm the story. The years of occurrence changed, and the number of participants involved varied. Sometimes, the direction of travel was different. But the stories began and ended essentially the same.

The starting points varied: Marshall, Hot Springs, or other places along the railroad. Collect calls made home asking for help from understanding uncles or older brothers were, fortunately, the outcomes of the Madison County boxcar adventures.

The many times I listened to variations in the story, the only constant I found was the lack of participation by young women. Did this show a lack of desire for adventure for the young women of Madison County? When I put these inquiries to the female peers of railway adventurers, the most common explanation I received was: "Girls just weren't that stupid."

My coauthor, who grew up in Barnard, told me of a neighbor there who, one sunny afternoon, decided to show several hangers-on how to catch a ride on a passing train. His plan was to grab one of the ladders on the end of a boxcar, swing up, and then jump off a few hundred yards from the railroad crossing.

He was a grown man in his 40s and a respected member of the community. Alas, he waited a bit too long, catching a boxcar near the end of the train. Having cleared the crossing, the train accelerated rapidly, and he could not get off safely.

He was not able to dismount until he reached Newport, TN, about 50 miles to the east. Undeterred, he bided his time until he could catch a westbound train. When the train rolled through Barnard, he again decided it was traveling too fast and found himself in Asheville. At this point, he decided to end this misadventure and called his wife, who drove up and got him.

The Pastor and the Hobo

While researching this subject, I came across the story of another 40-something, well-respected man who went on longer, more successful train-hopping excursions, possibly because he had a "professional" hobo to guide him. Compared to the spur-of-the-moment, unplanned trips already discussed, this one was a luxury junket. I'm not sure if that makes it better or worse. Anyway, it's too good a story not to tell.

In June 1980, 76-year-old Jack Randall led Reverend Willam Kirk of the Barrington United Methodist Church near Chicago and three of the pastor's friends on a five-day, 2,280-mile journey to Seattle.

In addition to the pastor and the hobo, the group included an airline pilot, an advertising agency art director, and a dentist. Kirk told a Chicago Sun-Times reporter that the group rode in boxcars, grain cars, gondolas, lumber flatbeds, piggybacks (that carry truck trailers), and empty auto carriers.

Randall had turned up at Kirk's church looking for work and got into the habit of returning each summer for a number of years. Enthralled by Randall's stories, Kirk eventually asked to tag along on a trip.

"Each of us took one small bag with one change of clothes," Kirk said. "Our rain gear consisted of heavy-gauge trash bags. For blankets, we used newspapers. We didn't carry any food or water but ate in restaurants during layovers. I took along $150. I also had my American Express card, mostly in case I needed bail money."

Kirk actually made it to his intended destination and had the most graceful return trip; he simply bought a plane ticket and flew home to Chicago. I can't help but wonder what his congregation thought of his illicit rail travel.

14. Literary Larceny:
The Biltmore Estate Book Thefts

Biltmore House Library. Photo by Warren LeMay
(Flickr: Public Domain).

"A thief believes everybody steals," — E. W. Howe, American novelist, and newspaper editor.

In May and June of 1980, all of Asheville was abuzz with excitement. Don Knotts and Tim Conway were in town to shoot a comedy mystery film, *The Private Eyes*, at the Biltmore Estate. Everyone involved was in for more surprises than they could have imagined.

During filming, the movie was best known for building a gas station so that it could be blown up for a gag in the film. Even more memorable was the stunt in which a 1936 Rolls-Royce crashed into the Biltmore Estate's Bass Pond. Think of these as impractical practical effects.

The car didn't sink bottom-down into the pond as planned but flipped over in the water and came to rest on the front of the roof. Stuntman Tommy Huff was trapped in the car for two or three minutes. He made it out OK with a cut ankle and a case of shock. They lifted the car out with a crane.

Six months later, the movie was famous for accidentally uncovering a multi-year scheme to steal rare books. That's right, a film about two bumbling detectives triggered a multi-state, if not an international, search for rare volumes and artifacts taken from the Biltmore Estate.

During a break in filming, a staff member offered to show Conway a rare book in the library. It was the 1856 edition of Samuel Johnson's *A Dictionary of the English Language*. When they opened the slip-case, which should have contained the two-volume set valued at $7,500, it was empty. An inventory showed that 234 rare books valued at over $300,000 were missing.

From *True Crime Stories of Western North Carolina* by Cathy Pickens:

> *"The staff called authorities, and in looking through the library, they found other treasures missing, among them Edmund Spenser's The Faerie Queene and an 1887 edition of Eadweard Muybridge's Animal Locomotion, a series of photographs demonstrating the first stop-action study of the movement of a running horse, valued at $100,000. The library was also missing rare volumes by Lewis Carroll, the Brothers Grimm, The Book of Common Prayer, and a portfolio of Goya etchings."*

In early July, Knotts, Conway, and the rest of the cast and crew flew back to the West Coast, focused on finishing the film, which hit theaters in November. Meanwhile, back at the 255-room Biltmore House, a careful, methodical investigation continued and was about to uncover a most unlikely culprit.

An Unexpected Villian

The thief was Robert Livingston Matters, a Harvard graduate with a master's degree in art who was formerly a college professor. He operated Plane Tree Book Service, an antique bookbinding shop in downtown Asheville. Matters also worked at the Biltmore Estate as a security guard under the name Rustem Levni Turkseven.

It appears he chose the Turkish alias because of his travels to Turkey, Greece, and Cyprus. He had a thorough understanding of the language and culture. Finally, his wife was Turkish. She had emigrated to the United States as a high school student. While he was exceptionally qualified to pull off this masquerade, it would have made him more memorable, not less.

On Tuesday, January 13, 1981, an FBI press conference introduced Robert Matters and Rustem Turkseven to the world. Matters had been tracked down in Washington, D.C., arrested, and brought to Asheville. He pleaded guilty to four counts of interstate transportation of stolen property.

FBI Special Agent Robert Pence said at one point, the investigation had involved 40 FBI agents. The theft was discovered on June 10. At the time of the January press conference, they had recovered 60 items. The FBI believed Matters had taken the books and other items between December 19, 1979, and May 12, 1980. Efforts to recover the remaining stolen items continued.

From *Lady on the Hill: How Biltmore Estate Became an American Icon* by Howard E. Covington Jr.:

> *"We found books all over the country," said William A.V. Cecil, owner of the Biltmore Estate at the time of the theft. "Bank of America bought one of our books from a dealer in Texas. So did someone in London. Sotheby's and Christie's said we can't check the provenance of every book. I said, 'Someone comes in from some little town called Asheville, which you have never heard of except it has a big old house named Biltmore, which you have heard of. And this kid comes in and says he runs a little bookstore and brings in twenty or thirty very valuable books with [a label reading] Ex Libris Biltmoris in there, and you don't check.'"*

It seems odd that Cecil referred to Matters as "this kid," considering that Matter was 56 at the time of the thefts, which made him four years older than Cecil.

It took over two years to recover the remaining books and works of art, most of which had been sold to rare books and art dealers. On March 3, 1981, Judge Woodrow Wilson Jones sentenced Matters to two concurrent five-year terms and two $5,000 fines.

The Private Eyes was a commercial success, making $12 million on a budget of $2.3 million. Many consider it a cult classic. It was the final time Conway and Knotts appeared in a film together, not counting their cameos as California Highway Patrol officers in Cannonball Run II, a movie so bad that we all agreed to pretend it never happened.

15. Deadly Drifter

A killer without a conscience or a plan.

Ghost Town in the Sky Entrance. Photo by Mike Burton
(Flickr: Used with Permission).

"Murder is unique in that it abolishes the party it injures, so that society has to take the place of the victim and on his behalf demand atonement or grant forgiveness; it is the one crime in which society has a direct interest." — W. H. Auden, British-American poet.

Friday, July 10, 1992, had been a hot, clear, breezy day with a high of 91°F (32.8°C) and winds up to 14 mph (23 kph) in Maggie Valley, N.C., about 35 miles (56 km) west of Asheville. A security guard, James Mathis, was doing his rounds an hour after Ghost Town in the Sky, a Wild West-themed amusement park atop Buck Mountain, closed. He discovered a drunk man hiding under a bus, called the Maggie Valley Police Department, and reported a trespasser.

Police Chief Saralyn Carver responded to the call. The man, James Neil Tucker, handed over his driver's license. She called it in to dispatch. When the dispatcher came back over the radio saying Tucker was wanted for murder in South Carolina. He pulled out a .25-caliber semiautomatic handgun and put it to Carver's head. Mathis moved fast, tackling Tucker and wrestling him to the ground.

"He was standing close enough to him where he grabbed his arm and threw a tackle on him at the same time. The guy dropped the gun, and they got the handcuffs on him," said Perry Littrell, park maintenance and security manager, in a telephone interview with the Associated Press.

Tucker had been on the run for 15 days. He was wanted in connection with the murders of Rosa Lee "Dolly" Oakley in Sumter, SC, and Sharon Lynn Mellon in St. Matthews. An elderly couple had seen him hitchhiking and given him a ride, never realizing they had a stone-cold killer in their backseat.

A Bizarre Burglary, Kidnapping, Murder

Tucker had been in and out of prison in Utah for rape, theft, and prison escapes. While incarcerated, he met an inmate from South Carolina. Tucker escaped again in 1983 and came to South Carolina, where he and his friend found work at a horse farm in Calhoun County southeast of Columbia.

Tucker, unable to stay out of trouble with the law, was arrested and convicted in Spartanburg for housebreaking and larceny and sentenced to 10 years. When he completed his South Carolina sentence, he returned to Utah to complete his unfinished sentence there.

He was paroled on August 27, 1991, and returned to South Carolina, this time to Sumter, where he found work as a welder at a metal products company. In March 1992, he married his girlfriend, Marcia, who had become pregnant. Tucker said that the pregnancy was the reason he embarked on a series of robberies and burglaries that led him to the home of 54-year-old Dolly Oakley.

> *"Seemed like every time I brought a paycheck home, I was further in debt, and that's why I started this whole thing," Tucker told police.*

On June 25, 1992, Tucker parked in the Oakley's driveway at about 10:00 a.m. and approached Dolly, who was working in her yard. After making certain that her husband wasn't home, he pulled out a gun and forced her into the house.

Joe Black knocked on the front door. He and James Howard had driven up looking for her husband, James. Tucker let her answer the door to tell them Mr. Oakley wasn't home. As they were backing down the driveway, she bolted from the house, screaming, "Don't leave me; he's going to kill me." They drove off quickly, went to a phone, and called the police. Both men knew Tucker; Sumter was a small town.

Tucker dragged her back into the house and bound her hands with tape. He then shot her in the head twice, stole money from her purse, and quickly left. Responding officers found her lying on the bed dead. They immediately began searching for Tucker, and his photo and full description were in the next day's newspaper.

The Chase Begins

On Sunday, June 27, at about 3:15 p.m., two women entered the Sumter Christian Fellowship Baptist Church. They were church members who had come to do some cleaning. In the kitchen area, they encountered Tucker eating some canned food. He had taken off his shirt and shoes to dry them and fled wearing only his jeans. He had gained entry by breaking a window.

Police converged on the church, and 50-75 officers with bloodhounds searched a 10-square-mile area. They found footprints behind a nearby junkyard but gave up the search at about 6 p.m. when it began to rain. Unknown to the officers, Tucker had hidden in the trunk of one of the junked cars and stayed concealed there for seven to eight hours.

Later, he broke into a nearby trailer and stole a shirt and some hiking boots. He then left Sumter, traveling in the back of a delivery truck, the bed of a pickup, and in a tire carrier underneath an 18-wheeler. Arriving in St. Mathews on July 1, he stole a station wagon from a funeral home. Tucker got the car stuck in a wooded area and walked to the cottage near Webb Carroll's Training Center, where Shannon Lynn Mellon was living while she trained to become a jockey. He was looking for another car.

A Chevy Blazer and a Ford Mustang were parked outside. Pressing his ear against the cottage wall, he could hear a man and a woman talking. Later in his confession, he stated that he intended to go inside, shoot them both, and take whatever money they had along with one of the vehicles.

Before he could put his plan into action, the man walked outside and drove off in the Blazer. He cut through a window screen, entered the house, tied Mellon up, went to the kitchen, got a glass of milk, came back, and shot her in the back of the head.

After a moment, she said, "I can't see." He shot her again. After packing up some items from the house, he heard her ragged breathing and shot her a third time in the temple. He rolled her body up in a sheet, covered the bloody mattress with a bedspread, and carried her about 100 yards out into the woods. He thought this would buy him some time; he was right.

He climbed into Mellon's 1989 Limited Edition Mustang and headed to Spartanburg, where he knew people from his earlier time in South Carolina. He hung out with acquaintances there for about a week who apparently didn't watch the news or read newspapers, then hitchhiked the 95 miles (150 km) to Maggie Valley to check out Ghost Town in the Sky.

On Friday, July 10, police found Mellon's car abandoned in a Piggly Wiggly parking lot in Spartanburg. Tucker had changed the license plate, but they determined the owner using the car's VIN number.

Unable to reach Mellon on the phone, Calhoun County deputies went to check on her. They found the phone line cut, blood on a mattress, and a bloody trail leading into the woods. They discovered her body wrapped in a sheet in a pine thicket. The search for James Neil Tucker went from red hot to white hot. Fortunately for everyone, he was captured before nightfall, trying to hide at the Western North Carolina amusement park.

The day after his arrest in Maggie Valley, Tucker gave a 48-page confession to South Carolina Law Enforcement Division (S.L.E.D.) Agent Perry Herod and Sumter County Sheriff's Detective Glenn Harrell.

The 35-year-old Tucker had been born in New Mexico but had spent most of his life in Utah. His mother had remarried, and his stepfather was physically abusive. At a young age, he began to commit petty crimes in an effort to get taken out of the home. In addition, Tucker claimed that he had been raped at age 13 while in a Utah state mental hospital.

In 1974, at 17, James Neil Tucker was sentenced to one to 15 years for the rape of an eight-year-old girl. He was also charged with the rape of an 83-year-old woman, but her family moved her to California and refused to let her return to testify.

Throughout Tucker's multiple prison terms in Utah from 1974 to 1991, he was cited for numerous prison rules and state law violations. These infractions ranged from being out of bounds to escape and included incidents of possessing makeshift weapons known as "shanks" and drug use.

He had served more than 13 years in prison, not counting his time in a South Carolina prison for the Spartanburg housebreaking. Before his murder trials, psychiatrists diagnosed Tucker with a severe antisocial personality disorder stemming from physical and sexual abuse.

The Trials of James Neil Tucker

Tucker had three trials. On Wednesday, December 8, 1993, a Calhoun County jury found him guilty of murder, armed robbery, first-degree burglary, and grand larceny of a vehicle in the killing of Shannon Mellon. He was sentenced to death.

A year later, on Friday, December 16, 1994, a Sumter County jury found him guilty of murder, kidnapping, first-degree burglary, armed robbery, and possession of a weapon during a violent crime in the killing of Dolly Oakley. Once more, he was sentenced to die.

The death sentence from the first trial was reversed due to a U.S. Supreme Court ruling that required courts to state whether or not parole was possible before a defendant could be sentenced to death. So, a third trial was held on July 17, 1996, in which a Calhoun County jury reimposed the death penalty. In all, 36 jurors had agreed that Tucker should die for his crimes.

On May 28, 2004, 12 years after he murdered Dolly Oakley, James Neil Tucker was executed at the Capital Punishment Facility in Columbia, S.C. At 6:00 p.m., the curtain between the death chamber and the witnesses opened, and Tucker was strapped into the electric chair; a brown hood was placed over his head, and an electrician checked the connections.

At 6:04, with an audible "thump," a breaker fell, and Tucker's body jerked upward; then the breaker was opened, and he slumped forward in the restraints. A few seconds later, the breaker closed again, and more current coursed through his body for about two minutes. There was no reaction. He was pronounced dead at 6:11 p.m. Oakley's husband and Mellon's father attended the execution.

Richard Walker, Orangeburg Times and Democrat staff writer, in his May 23, 2004, article, Portrait of a Killer, wrote:

"Former 1st Circuit Solicitor Walter Bailey, who prosecuted Tucker's case, and James 'Jay' Jackson, Tucker's lead defense counsel, have contrasting opinions about who he (Tucker) is: a cold-hearted, calculating serial killer or a misguided man overcome by the grim circumstances of his life. Bailey said the Utah man is nothing short of an intelligent yet evil monster with little emotion who deserves his fate for killing the two women. Jackson says that given different circumstances, Tucker could have been a positive leader in any given community."

It is the opinion of my cowriter and I that both Bailey and Jackson might have been right.

Help Us Bring These Stories to New Readers

Review the Book Today!

We greatly appreciate the time you took to read *Blood on the Blue Ridge*. As indie authors, it means a lot, and we hope our book has brought these mountain stories to life!

If you can spare a moment or two, please leave a review or rating on Amazon. It helps us gain more readers and keep these stories and Appalachian history alive. Plus, we love learning which stories resonated with you! Every review makes a world of difference.

To leave your feedback:

1. Open your camera app.

2. Point your mobile device at the QR code below.

3. The review page will appear in your web browser.

Thank you!

R. Scott Lunsford and Alfred Dockery

Sources
The Nearly Fatal Footprint

Forster Alexander Sondley, *A History of Buncombe County, North Carolina* (Advocate Printing Company, 1930), 472-73, 750–51.

Forster Alexander Sondley, *Asheville and Buncombe County* (The Inland Press, Asheville, N.C., 1922). 86

John Preston Arthur, *Western North Carolina: A History (From 1730-1913)* (Raleigh, N.C., Edwards & Broughton Printing Company, 1914). 379, 389-90,

Anne E Chesky, *Riceville* (Arcadia Publishing, 2011). 8

1808 Correspondence of Governor Benjamin Williams available online at North Carolina Digital Collections

Raleigh Minerva, Thursday, April 07, 1808, Page 3, "Communication" Item dated 25th March.

Raleigh Minerva, Tuesday, April 12, 1808, Page 3, "Raleigh" Column dated May 12.

Raleigh Minerva, Thursday, April 21, 1808, Page 3, "Raleigh" Item dated April 10.

Richmond Enquirer, VA, Saturday, May 14, 1808, Page 2 "Raleigh, (N.C.) Item dated May 5 has the notation: [Register. at the bottom.

Raleigh Minerva, Thursday, May 26, 1808, Page 2, "Raleigh"

Weekly Raleigh Register, Thursday, May 26, 1808, Page 3, "Raleigh"

Wilson's Knoxville Gazette, TN, Wednesday, July 27, 1808, Page 3, "Take Notice !!"

Asheville Citizen-Times, Monday, March 03, 2014, Page D4, "Historic: Large Trove" By Rob Neufeld (Visiting Our Past)

Asheville Citizen-Times, Monday, March 24, 2014, Page D1, "West the Innocence Project of 1808 in Asheville" By Rob Neufeld (Visiting Our Past)

Asheville Citizen-Times, Monday, September 16, 2019, Page A3, "From an 1808 Murder to a New Development, the Story Continues"

The Hermit of Bald Mountain

Lanman, Charles. *Letters from the Allegheny Mountains*. United States: Geo. Putnam, 1849.

Zeigler, Wilbur G, and Ben S Grosscup. 1883. *The Heart of the Alleghanies*; Or, Western North Carolina. A. Williams & Company.

Arthur, John Preston. *Western North Carolina: A History (1730-1913)*. United States: Edwards & Broughton Printing Company, 1914.

Inscoe, John C. *Mountain Masters: Slavery, and the Sectional Crisis in Western North Carolina.* United States: University of Tennessee Press, 1996.

Hsiung, David C. *Two Worlds in the Tennessee Mountains*: Exploring the Origins of Appalachian Stereotypes. United States: University Press of Kentucky, 2021.

Alderman, Pat. *Wonders of the Unakas Unicoi County*. United States: Erwin Business and Professional Women's Club, 1964.

Alderman, Pat. *Greasy Cove in Unicoi County*: Authentic Folklore. United States: Overmountain Press, 1975.

Daily National Intelligencer and Washington Express, D.C., Friday, January 14, 1825, Page 3, News Item

Morning Chronicle, London, England · Friday, January 28, 1825, Page 3 "Horrid Murder"

Raleigh Register, NC, Friday, February 11, 1825, Page 1 "Murder"

Constitutional Whig, Richmond, VA, Friday, May 06, 1825, Page 3 "Trial for Murder"

Alexandria Gazette, VA, Tuesday, May 10, 1825, Page 3 "An Extraordinary Man"

Raleigh Morning Post, Sunday, September 6, 1903, Page 13, "Spill-Corn Laurel and Its Lawyers" by Bud Wuntz (John Preston Arthur)

Knoxville Sentinel, Tuesday, April 10, 1917, Page 6 "Hermit of the Bald"

Asheville Citizen-Times, Sunday, November 23, 1952, Page 26, "Greer Bald is Monument to Hermit" by C. R. Sumner

Johnson City Press, TN, Tuesday, November 09, 1965, Page 10, "Time Finally Deals Out Its Appropriate Justice" by Dorothy Hamill

Johnson City Press, TN, Sunday, February 28, 1971, Page 27, "Love Struck a Cruel Blow to Bald Mountain Hermit" by Jimmy Neil Smith

Asheville Citizen, Thursday, January 29, 1976, Page 1, "King of the Mountain, Hermit Proclaimed" By John Parris

The Unconquerable Nancy Franklin

Dean, Nadia. *Murder in the Mountains: Historic true crime in Western North Carolina.* Cherokee, NC: Valley River Press, 2021.

Inscoe, John C., and Gordon B. McKinney. *The Heart of Confederate Appalachia: Western North Carolina in the Civil War.* Chapel Hill, NC: University of North Carolina Press, 2003.

Paludan, P.S. (1981) *Victims: A true story of the Civil War.* Knoxville, TN: University of Tennessee Press.

Trotter, William R. *Bushwhackers! The Civil War in North Carolina.* Winston-Salem, NC: John F. Blair, 1988.

Wellman, Manly Wade. *The Kingdom of Madison: A southern mountain fastness and its people.* Alexander, NC: Land of the Sky Books, 2001.

Asheville News, Thursday, May 25, 1854, Page 3, "Stop the Murders" by A. E. Baird, Lapland, NC.

Fayetteville Observer (Semi-Weekly), Monday, April 23, 1855, Page 3, "Superior Court,"

Memphis Bulletin, TN, Wednesday, July 15, 1863, Page 2, "Rebel Outrages in East Tennessee"

Daily Confederate, Raleigh, Thursday, June 30, 1864, Page 2, "Affairs in Madison County"

Daily Confederate, Raleigh, Thursday, August 18, 1864, Page 2, Account of Major Charles Roberts' successful raid into East Tennessee. It references Asheville News.

The Daily Progress, Raleigh, NC, Thursday, October 06, 1864, Page 1, "Death of Major Roberts" Item picked up from the Asheville News.

Charlotte Democrat, Tuesday, October 11, 1864, Page 1, Notice of the death of Major Charles Roberts of the 14th Cavalry Battalion, formerly Woodfin's Battalion, after a raid on a house on Laurel. It references the Asheville News of September 29.

M. E. Weeks, pension examiner, February 17, 1875, letter to James H. Baker, Commissioner of Pensions. (Slagle)

Union and American, Greeneville, Tennessee, Thursday, August 17, 1876, Page 2, "George Franklin vs Nancy Franklin"

State vs. James Shelton, NC Supreme Court August Term 1855. North Carolina Digital Collections, Page 360 (Page 368-373 of the digital record.) Per Curiam. Judgment reversed and a venire de novo.

October 4, 1883, George Norton deposition to Howard Miller, Special Examiner of the Pension Office. (Slagle)

April 20, 1886, House Report on Nancy Franklin (No. 1793)

June 5, 1886, Congressional Record - Senate H. R. 7365 for the relief of Nancy Franklin passes

News and Observer, Raleigh, November 18, 1956, Page 29, "With Your Teeth in a Throat" by Manly Wade Wellman

Asheville Citizen-Times, Sunday, April 26, 1959, Page 35, "Revenge Dear for Nancy Norton" by Beale Fletcher

Our State magazine, April 29, 2012, Atrocity at Shelton Laurel by Philip Gerard

Thomas Strange: Wealth, Power, and a Murder in Appalachia

Arthur, John Preston. *Western North Carolina: A History (1730-1913).* United States: Edwards & Broughton Printing Company, 1914.

The Living Present, Warrenton, NC, Friday, September 03, 1869, Page 3, "Strange Sentence"

Wilmington Journal, Friday, September 17, 1869, Page 1, "Judge Watts on His High Horse Again"

Asheville News, Friday, September 17, 1869, Page 2, "Our Botany Bay"

Charlotte Observer, Tuesday, August 24, 1875, Page 1, "Destressing Homicide in Haywood County—Two Wilmingtonians Arrested"

Asheville Citizen, Thursday, May 4, 1876, Pages 2, 7, 6, 3, "The Strange-Murray Homicide."

Charlotte Observer, Saturday, May 06, 1876, Page 4, "The Last of the Strange-Murray Homicide" (Quotes Judge Watts' Written Instructions to the Jury)

Charlotte Democrat, Monday, May 22, 1876, Page 2, "Indignation Meeting" (Reprint of Asheville Pioneer article)

Raleigh Sentinel, Tuesday, July 11, 1876, Page 2, "Another Judicial Outrage."

The Torchlight, Oxford, NC, Tuesday, July 18, 1876, Page 2, "Greasy Watts and the Supreme Court"

The North Carolinian, Elizabeth City, NC, Wednesday, October 26, 1898, Page 8, "Thomas W. Strange"

Wilmington Morning Star, NC, Wednesday, August 23, 1899, Page 1, "Col. T. W. Strange"

Asheville Citizen-Times, Sunday, February 22, 1953, Page 8B, "The Strange Case, One of WNC's Most Celebrated Homicides" by C. R. Sumner

Raleigh News and Observer, Saturday, January 27, 1979, Page 4, "Chief Justice as Highwayman"

Defiant Distillers: Stirring Up Trouble
Lewis Redmond

Stewart, Bruce, *King of the Moonshiners: Lewis R. Redmond in Fact and Fiction* (Knoxville, TN: University of Tennessee Press, 2008)

Arthur, John Preston, *Western North Carolina: A History from 1730-1913* (Raleigh, NC: Edwards & Broughton Printing Co., 1914)

Tinsley, Jim Bob, *The Land of Waterfalls*: Transylvania County, North Carolina (Brevard, NC: J.B. and Dottie Tinsley, 1988)

Cobb, Robert A., *The True Life of Maj. Lewis Richard Redmond*, the Notorious Outlaw and Famous Moonshiner (Raleigh, NC: Edwards & Broughton Printing Co., 1881)

Carolina Watchman, Salisbury, NC, Thursday, March 09, 1876, Page 3, "A U.S. Deputy Marshal Killed"

Pickens Sentinel, SC, Thursday, January 18, 1887 "Shooting Affray"

Intelligencer, Anderson, SC, Thursday, July 11, 1878, Page 1 "Redmond's Strange Story"

Greenville News, SC, Friday, August 26, 1881 "To 10 Charges"

Intelligencer, Anderson, SC, Thursday, May 22, 1884, Page 2 "A Pardon for Redmond"

Newberry Herald and News, SC, Thursday, October 27, 1887, Page 3, "Redmond's Handmade Corn Whiskey"

Arch Babb

Atlanta Journal, Wednesday, January 22, 1902, Page 7, "Brothers-in-Law Fight, One Killed, One Wounded"

Asheville Citizen, Wednesday, January 22, 1902, Page 3, "Partners Fight Over Distillery"

Madison County Record, Marshall, Friday, January 24, 1902, Page 4 "A Tragedy on Shut In"

The News and Observer, Friday, January 24, 1902, Page 3, "Shot Down at a Still"

The Morning Post, Raleigh, Thursday, September 22, 1904, Page 3, "Babb Held for Murder"

Madison County Record, Marshall, Friday, March 10, 1905, Page 6, Brief item, No headline

Garrett Hedden

Hubbard, Jr., Leonidas. "The Moonshiner at Home." The Atlantic, August 1902.

Tennessean, Nashville, Wednesday, November 09, 1898, Page 3, "Killed His Brother"

Daily Times, Chattanooga, Wednesday, November 09, 1898, Page 5, "Polk County Tragedy"

Knoxville Sentinel, Friday, November 18, 1898, Page 7, "Fratricide"

Journal and Tribune, Knoxville, Friday, August 17, 1900, Page 5, "Biggest Revenue Raid Made in Some Years"

Tennessean, Nashville, Tuesday, August 21, 1900, Page 3, "Fusillade on Frog Mountain"

Morristown Republican, TN, Saturday, August 25, 1900, Page 1 "Moonshine Raid"

Chattanooga Daily Times, Sunday, January 05, 1908, Page 4, "Fratricide Meets Doom"

Atlanta Constitution, Sunday, January 05, 1908, Page 1, "Noted Outlaw Killed by Posse"

Knoxville Journal and Tribune, Sunday, January 05, 1908, Page 1, "Noted Moonshiner and Outlaw Killed"

Knoxville Sentinel, Thursday, January 09, 1908, Page 5, "Tell of Killing Garrett Hedden"

Nashville Banner, Sunday, June 15, 1924, Page 1, "Red Record of Hedden Boys"

Josiah "Joe Banty" Gregory

Dunn, D. (1988). *Cades Cove the Life and Death of a Southern Appalachian Community*, 1818-1937 (pp. 232–240). University of Tennessee Press.

Oliver, W. W. (2014) *Cades Cove: A Personal History* (pp. 113-120), Great Smoky Mountain Association.

Knoxville Sentinel, Tuesday, December 27, 1921, Page 5 "Cade's Cove Man May Not Survive Wounds"

Knoxville Journal and Tribune, Tuesday, December 27, 1921, Page 12, "Quarrel Ends in Shooting"

Journal and Tribune, Knoxville, 08 Feb 1922, Wed, Page 5 "Gregories Held; Arson Charged"

Journal and Tribune, Knoxville, 06 Jul 1922, Thu, Page 5 "Liquor Sellers In Hard Lines"

Knoxville Sentinel 21 Oct 1922, Sat, Page 2 "Two Convicted Burning Barn in Blount County"

Journal and Tribune, Knoxville, Thursday, November 02, 1922, Page 5 "Busy Term of Court at Maryville"

Chattanooga News, 24 Dec 1923, Mon, Page 12 "Gov. Peay Grants Holiday Pardons"

Ike Strong

Lexington Herald-Leader, Thursday, March 29, 1923, Page 3, "Four Killed in Leslie Co. Fight"

Owensboro Messenger-Inquirer, Thursday, March 29, 1923, Page 1, "Moonshiners in Desperate Last Stand Battle"

Middlesboro Daily News, Thursday, March 29, 1923, Page1, "Four Lose Lives in Leslie County Moonshine Raid"

Frankfort State Journal, Sunday, April 01, 1923, Page 1, "Moonshiners Die Defending Fort"

The 33-Year Fugitive

US Census 1910, Police Jury Ward 6, Calcasieu, LA

US Census 1930, DeQuincy, Calcasieu, LA

Asheville Daily Gazette, Sunday, September 2, 1900, Page 8, News Item

Raleigh Morning Post, Sunday, September 2, 1900, Page 6, "Shooting Affair Which is Expected to Result Fatally"

Asheville Semi-Weekly Citizen, Tuesday, June 18, 1901, Page 4, "Three Capital Cases on Docket for Trial"

Asheville Citizen, Tuesday, October 15, 1901, Page 4, $200 Reward for James Lunsford

Statesville Landmark, NC, Tuesday, February 11, 1908, Page 2, "A Brutal Wife Murder in Madison"

French Broad News, Marshall, NC, Thursday, August 27, 1908, Page 3, "Randall Gets 30 Years"

Raleigh News and Observer, Friday, October 27, 1933, "Seeks Trial for Slaying in 1900"

Monroe News-Star, LA, Friday, October 27, 1933, Page 1, "Rancher is Back in Native Hills to Stand Trial"

Asheville Times, Saturday, October 28, 1933, Page 8, "Self-Defense Will be Plea in Murder Case"

Asheville Citizen, Wednesday, August 29, 1934, Page 11, "Lunsford to Face Trial in Slaying Case Today"

Asheville Citizen, Wednesday, December 26, 1934, Page 1, "Madison Farmer is Gun Victim"

Greensboro Daily News, Monday, August 26, 1935, Page 5, "Courts May Reopen Old Mountain Feud"

Raleigh News and Observer, Friday, August 30, 1935, Page 2, "Nol Pros is Taken in Old Murder Case"

Atlanta Constitution, Saturday, August 31, 1935, Page 6, "Man Freed in Carolina in 35-year-old Killing"

A Life in Liquor and Blood

State v. Exum, 138 N.C. 599 (1905) March 21, 1905, Supreme Court of North Carolina 138 N.C.

Statesville Record and Landmark, Tuesday, January 19, 1904, Page 3, News Item

Nashville Graphic, NC, Thursday, January 21, 1904, Page 1, "Murder at Hot Springs"

Gaffney Ledger, SC, Friday, January 22, 1904, Page 1, "Throughout the Tarheel State"

Madison County Record, Marshall, NC, Friday, January 22, 1904, Fri Page 3, "Killing at Hot Springs"

Raleigh Morning Post, Tuesday, February 09, 1904, Page 2, "Judge Long Makes a Severely Plain Talk from the Bench"

Charlotte Observer, Saturday, March 05, 1904, Page 3, "Madison Court Kept Busy"

Raleigh News and Observer, Saturday, March 05, 1904, Page 1, "Nine Murder Cases"

Raleigh Morning Post, Friday, January 22, 1904, Page 8, "Postscripts"

Raleigh Morning Post, Saturday, September 09, 1905, Page 5, "Fred Avery"

Winston-Salem Union Republican, Thursday, September 14, 1905, Page 3, "Peter Smith to Hang"

Raleigh News and Observer, Tuesday, September 25, 1906, Page 5, "Fred Avery Pardoned"

Asheville Citizen, Saturday, June 01, 1912, Page 6, "Will Maxwell Shot: Instantly Killed"

Asheville Gazette-News, Saturday, June 01, 1912, Page 3, "Negro Kills Another and Makes his Escape"

Danville Bee, VA, Saturday, January 20, 1934, Page 2, "Autopsy Evidence More Reliable Than X-Ray in Local Murder Case"

Danville Bee, VA, Wednesday, March 14, 1934, Page 1, "Fuller Geta a 10 Year Term for Homicide"

Peter Smith: A Controversial Hanging

State vs. Smith, 138 N.C. 700 (1905) (Transcript)

State v. Stines, 138 N.C. 686 (1905) May 23, 1905, NC Supreme Court

Rusher, James Thomas. "Case III: The Trouble with Hanging." *Until He Is Dead: Capital Punishment in the Western North Carolina History*, Parkway Publishers, Boone, NC, 2003, pp. 140, 152, 155, 158, 161, 162, 166.

Charlotte News, Wednesday, November 13, 1901, Page 2, "For the Murder of His Stepdaughter"

Madison County Record (Marshall, NC), Friday, March 17, 1905, Page 4, "Peter Smith"

Raleigh Morning Post, Tuesday, August 1, 1905, Page 5, "Charlie Stines Will Not Hang"

Winston-Salem Union Republican, Thursday, August 17, Page 3, "Rape Should Mean Rope"

Raleigh News and Observer, Saturday, September 9, 1905, Page 5, "Gallows Waits for Peter Smith"

Asheville Citizen, Tuesday, September 19, 1905, Page 1, "Girls Testimony Robs Peter Smith of a Final Chance to Escape Death"

Raleigh Morning Post, Thursday, September 21, 1905, Page 2, "Peter Smith's Victim Insisted on Being Locked in Cell in Asheville"

Asheville Citizen, Tuesday, October 03, 1905, Page 1, "Standing on the Shores of Eternity Peter Smith, Hanged Yesterday at Marshall, Declared his Innocence"

Wadesboro Messenger and Intelligencer, NC, Thursday, October 05, 1905, Page 2, "For Criminal Assault Peter Smith Was Hanged"

Madison County Record, Friday, October 06, 1905, Page 5, "Execution of Peter Smith"

Greensboro Daily News, Saturday, June 10, 1911, Page 3, "Gave Him Freedom"

Raleigh News and Observer, Saturday, June 10, 1911, Page 5, "Charlie Stines First Sentenced to Death, for Rape, His Sentence Commuted to Life Imprisonment is Now Set Free"

Murderous Manhunts: Will Harris and Broadus Miller

State v Mansell, 192 N. C. 20, 133 S. E. 190 (1926)

Will Harris

Charlotte News, Saturday, July 23, 1904, Page 2 "The Negro Detective, Van Griffin, is Dead" (Note: Article includes a photo of Will Harris.)

Asheville Citizen, Wednesday, November 14, 1906, Page 1 "Brave City Officers Fall Dead on Streets Acting in the Line of Duty"

Farmer and Mechanic, Raleigh, Tuesday, November 20, 1906, Page 3 "Desperado Game to the Last Ditch"

Statesville Landmark, Tuesday, November 20, 1906, Page 1 "The Man Not Will Harris"

Asheville Citizen, Saturday, November 17, 1906, Page 1 "Avengers are Commended by Harris' Jury"

Broadus Miller

Blood in the Hills: A History of Violence in Appalachia. United States: University Press of Kentucky, 2012. Chapter 12. "The Largest Manhunt in Western North Carolina History": The Story of Broadus Miller, pages 340-379 by Kevin W. Young.

Kevin W. Young, "*The World of Broadus Miller:* Homicide, Lynching and Outlawry in Early Twentieth-Century North and South Carolina," (University of Georgia, 2016).

Young, Kevin W. "*The Murder of Gladys Kincaid*: The Story Behind the Ballads." North Carolina Folklore Journal, 2009, 21–32. https://digital.ncdcr.gov/digital/collection/p16062coll43/id/8487.

The State, Columbia, SC, Thursday, January 21, 1904, Page 7 "Sheriff's Report on Dorchester Lynching"

The State, Columbia, SC, Tuesday, May 3, 1921, Page 2 "Negro Boy Slays Aged Negro Woman"

Watchman and Southron, Sumter, SC, Saturday, May 07, 1921, Page 4 "Brutal Murder in Anderson"

Asheville Citizen, Sunday, September 20, 1925, Page 1 "Sheriff Takes Negro from the City as Big Crowd Begins to Form"

Charlotte Observer, Monday, September 21, 1925, Page 1 "Negro Suspect Brought Here from Asheville"

Asheville Citizen, Tuesday, October 27, 1925, Page 1 "Police Arrest negro for Attack on Woman While Crowd Waits for Word from Assailant of Another"

News and Observer, Raleigh, Saturday, June 25, 1927, Page 1 "Wrong Man may be Serving Time"

Winston-Salem Journal, Tuesday, June 28, 1927, Page 16 "Broadus Miller Still at Large"

Greensboro Daily News, Thursday, June 30, 1927, Page 1 "Negro Brute is Now Reported Only a Few Paces Ahead of Posse"

Charlotte News, Monday, July 4, 1927, Page 1 "Negro Outlaw Shot to Death in Mountains"

Statesville Landmark, Monday, July 4, 1927, Page 1 "Broadus Miller Killed in Gun Duel," "Broadus Miller's Body Buried Here"

News and Observer, Raleigh, Wednesday, July 06, 1927, Page 9 "Bridges Reports on Miller Death"

Charlotte Observer, Friday, July 15, 1927, Page 1, "Burleson in Bitter Reply to Attackers"

Watauga Democrat, Boone, Thursday, July 21, 1927, Page 1 "Dula Says Negro was Unarmed," "Man says Broad Miller Shot While Sleeping"

Charlotte Observer, Wednesday, August 3, 1927, "Gragg Denies He Instigated Burleson Row"

Watauga Democrat, Thursday, September 1, 1927, Page 1 "Burleson Settles $30,000 Damage Suit for One Cent"

News and Observer, Saturday, September 3, 1927, Page 2, "Desire Burleson to Divide Reward"

Charlotte Observer, Sunday, June 17, 1928, Page 2 "Death Reward Baffles Jury"

Montford Murders

Asheville Times, Monday, January 25, 1926, Page 1 "Burgess Case to Grand Jury Soon, is Belief

Asheville Times, Thursday, February 11, 1926, Page 1 "Frees Caleb Ingram and Bonnie Ledford in Burgess Murder

Asheville Citizen, Saturday, March 13, 1926, Page 2 "Davis Freed of Murder Charges"

Asheville Citizen, Wednesday, May 11, 1927, Page 1 "Cooper Death was Suicide Police Think"

Asheville Times, Friday, May 13, 1927, Page 1 "Mrs. Cooper was Murdered"

Asheville Times, Sunday, May 15, 1927, Page 1 "Police Center Investigation on Mrs. Montague"

Asheville Citizen, Wednesday, February 01, 1928, Page 1 "Nurse is Freed; Cooper Slaying Still Mystery"

The Great West Virginia Train Robbery

U.S. Postal Service. 1916. Photographs, Descriptions, and Records of Persons Charged with Violation of the Postal Laws. Vol. 1–2. Washington D.C.: U.S. Postal Service. (Harrison and Webb photos and descriptions in Volume 1; Diez in Volume 2.)

Atlanta Constitution, Wednesday, February 08, 1893, Page 3, "The Entire Gang of North Georgia Train Robbers has been Caught."

Birmingham News, AL, Monday, April 03, 1893, Page 6, "For Life, Jeff Harrison Sentenced to Anamosa"

Eufaula Times and News, AL, Thursday, May 04, 1893, Page 4, "Convicted Again"

Montgomery Weekly Advertiser, Friday, May 05, 1893, Page 6, News item regarding Harrison's second life sentence

Arlington Enterprise, KS, Friday, October 19, 1900, Page 4, "Two Sentences"

Atlanta Journal, Wednesday, June 13, 1900, Page 10, "Pardon for Train Robber Rewards Sister's Efforts"

Fairmont West Virginian, Saturday, October 09, 1915, Page 1, "Robbers Force U.S. Mail Clerks to Abandon Car"

Doddridge County Republican, WV, Thursday, October 14, 1915, "Great Train Robbery at Central Station"

Austin American, TX, Friday, March 24, 1916, "Notorious Train Robber Confesses; Arrested in S.A."

Martinsburg Evening Journal, WV, Wednesday, September 13, 1916, Page 1, Banner Headline, "Jeff Harrison Pleads Guilty and Gets 12 Years in Atlanta Penitentiary"

Beckley Raleigh Register, WV, Thursday, September 21, 1916, "Mystery of Train Robbery Cleared Up in Confession"

Sheboygan Press, WI, Monday, October 02, 1916, Page 2, "Harrison's Confession of Holdup Clears Up Crimes" by Harvey A. Bush.

Kansas City Journal, MO, Wednesday, January 17, 1917, Page 10, "Student Accused as Bank Robber"

Montgomery Advertiser, AL, Wednesday, April 04, 1917, Page 1, "Grady Webb Enters Plea of Guilty"

Washington Post, DC, Sunday, April 08, 1917, Page 5, "Sentence of Mail Robbers Breaks up Gang that was Long Terror of the South"

Charlotte Observer, Friday, April 13, 1917, Page 6, "H. Grady Webb was Arrested at Badin"

Keowee Courier, Pickens, SC, Wednesday, January 05, 1921, Page 4, "Train Robber Edits Paper"

Knoxville Journal, Tuesday, February 07, 1928, Page 1, "Paroled Convict May Become Rich Result Sentence"

Beckley Register and Post-Herald, WV, Saturday, June 22, 1963, Page 4, "Last Big Train Robbery in State in 1915" by Shirley Donnelly

A Deadly Reunion at Runion

State v. Frank Henderson and Gertrude Sams: Superior Court of Madison County transcript

State v. Frank Henderson: Supreme Court of North Carolina Date published: Dec 1, 1920, Opinion (Filed 24 December 1920.)

1920 Census Marshall Township Precinct 2

1930 Census Walnut (Village)

Asheville Citizen, Wednesday, August 25, 1920, Page 2, "Children Awake to Find Mother on Porch Dead"

Asheville Citizen, Monday, August 30, 1920, Page 12, "Frank Henderson of Madison, Confesses to Killing His Wife"

Asheville Citizen, Sunday, October 03, 1920, Page 12, "Frank Henderson Sentenced to be Electrocuted for Uxoricide"

Raleigh News and Observer, Sunday, October 03, 1920, Page 16, "Death Sentence for Killing Wife"

Winston-Salem Journal, Tuesday, October 12, 1920, Page 9, "Wife Murderer is Taken to Raleigh"

Charlotte Observer, Friday, September 16, 1921, Page 9, "No Pardon for Wife Murderer"

Charlotte Observer, Tuesday, October 11, 1921, Page 1, "Condemned Man Writes Letter as Final Task" by Brock Barkley

Raleigh News and Observer, Tuesday, October 11, 1921, Page 16, "Wife Slayer Pays Penalty for Crime"

Raleigh News and Observer, Friday, January 06, 1922, Page 7, "Bloodhound in Role of Wife Restorer in Mountain County"

The Old Money Murder

Asheville Citizen, NC, Monday, March 13, 1939, Page 1, "Believe Elderly Man, Who Resided Alone, was Robbed"

Morristown Gazette Mail, TN, Monday, March 13, 1939, Page 1, "Called to Help Find Murders"

Knoxville Journal, Knoxville, TN, Wednesday, March 15, 1939, Page 1 "Two Youths Laden with Cash, Jailed in Murder"

Asheville Citizen, NC, Thursday, March 16, 1939, Page 1, 3, "Youth Confesses Brutal Slaying of Aged Recluse"

Waynesville Mountaineer, NC, Thursday, March 16, 1939, Page 1, "Two Madison Boys Spent 5 Days Her After Alleged Theft"

Johnson City Chronicle, Friday, March 17, 1939, Page 3, "Mistake in Exchanging Hats Points to Solution of Death"

Charlotte Observer, NC, Thursday, May 25, 1939, Page 11, "Murder Trial is Under Way"

Asheville Times, NC, Thursday, May 25, 1939, Page 1, "Defense and State Rest in Duckett Case"

Asheville Citizen, NC, Friday, May 26, 1939, Page 1, 3, Page 1, "Murder Trial is Voided by Court Error"

Asheville Citizen, NC, Tuesday, November 28, 1939, Page 8, "Ducketts to be Tried for Alleged Murder of Ledford"

Asheville Times, NC, Friday, December 1, 1939, Page 9, "Ducket Youth Goes on Stand in Murder Trial in Madison"

Asheville Times, NC, Saturday, December 02, 1939, Page 1, "2 Ducketts Get 30 Years Each in Murder Case"

News and Observer, Raleigh, NC, Sunday, December 03, 1939, Page 5, "Convict Cousins On Murder Count"

Wilmington Morning Star, NC, Friday, September 20, 1940, Page 7, "Caledonia Guard Wounds Convict"

Skyland Post, West Jefferson, NC, Thursday, September 17, 1942, Page 1, "9 Watauga Escaped Convicts are Still Evading Officers"

News and Observer, Raleigh, NC, Wednesday, June 27, 1945, Page 8, "Pair Sentenced in Murder Case"

Reidsville Review, Friday, September 24, 1948, Page 1 (Doyle Duckett recaptured in Texas)

News and Observer, Raleigh, NC, Sunday, April 30, 1950, "Two Fugitives Back After Fleeing Camp"

Durham Sun, NC, Friday, December 04, 1953, Page 19, "State Grants 8 Paroles"

News and Observer, Raleigh, NC, Thursday, March 05, 1959, Page 20, "Paroles Given 17 Prisoners"

The Dangerous Pastime of Freighthopping

Freighthopping. Wikipedia

Federal Railroad Administration

Operation Lifesaver, Inc. (OLI) is a non-profit organization for rail safety education.

Chattanooga Times, Sunday, June 24, 1962, Page 17, "Medical History Made When Boy's Severed Arm Rejoined to Body"

Boston Globe, Wednesday, March 10, 1971, Page 3, "Four Years Later, a Carpenter Restores Old Life with New Hand"

Durham Morning Herald, Saturday, August 2, 1980, page 9, "Once a Year, Pastor Rides Rails with his Hobo Friend"

Mountain Xpress, July 7, 2016, "Off the Beaten Track: Freight Trains, Freedom and the Traveling Culture" by Max Hunt

Literary Larceny: The Biltmore Estate Book Thefts

Pickens, Cathy. *True Crime Stories of Western North Carolina*. Arcadia Publishing, 2022.

Covington, Howard E. *Lady on the Hill*: How Biltmore Estate Became an American Icon. John Wiley & Sons, 2006.

Moline Dispatch, IL, Saturday, June 02, 1956, Page 8, "Nilgul Muldur Betrothed"

Chicago Tribune, Monday, November 22, 1965, Page 16, "Turkey's Case in Cyprus" by Robert L. Matters

Asheville Citizen, Thursday, May 22, 1980, Page 20, "Arnold Explains Alda's WNC Movie"

Asheville Citizen, Monday, May 26, 1980, Page 1, "The Private Eyes Taking Over" by Tony Brown

Asheville Citizen, Tuesday, July 01, 1980, Page 1, "Stuntman Escapes Disaster" by Tony Brown

Asheville Times, Sunday, July 06, 1980, "Private Eyes, Movie is Now in the Can" by Bob Terrell

Asheville Citizen, Friday, November 07, 1980, Page 17, "Beauty and the Beast Return" by Bob Terrell

Asheville Citizen, Tuesday, January 13, 1981, Page 1, "Plea Filed; Rare Books Recovered" by Tony Brown

Charlotte Observer, Tuesday, January 13, 1981, Page 13, "Former Guard at Biltmore Pleads Guilty" by Jim Dumbell

Journal News, White Plains, NY, Tuesday, January 13, 1981, Page 2, "Guard Pleads Guilty to Rare Book Theft" (AP Story)

Asheville Citizen, Tuesday, March 03, 1981, Page 12, "Book Theft Nets Five-Year Term" By Tony Brown

Deadly Drifter

Jones, Mark R. 2007. *Palmetto Predators: Monsters Among Us*. Charleston, SC: History Press.

Salt Lake Tribune, Salt Lake City, Monday, December 07, 1981, Page 15, "Rape Convict Escapes Utah Prison"

The Item, Sumter, SC, Friday, June 26, 1992, Page 1, "Woman Murdered; Killer on the Loose" by Bonnie Blackburn and Eileen Waddell

The Item, Sumter, SC, Sunday, June 28, 1992, Page 1, "Lawmen Mount Search" by Lisa Dwyer-Dantzler and Billy Quarles

The Item, Sumter, SC, Friday, July 10, 1992, Page 1, "Tucker Linked to Second Murder"

Charlotte Observer, Saturday, July 11, 1992, Page 35, "Police Capture Man Suspected of Killing 2" AP

Winston-Salem Journal, NC, Sunday, July 12, 1992, Page 54, "Police Chief has Gun Pulled on Her in Park" AP

The State, Columbia, SC, Wednesday, July 15, 1992, Page 7, "Murder Suspect had 'No Regard for Laws,' Deputy Says" by Nina Brook

The Item, Sumter, SC, Thursday, September 24, 1992, Page 1, "Tucker Suicide Attempt Suspected" by Bonnie Blackburn

The State, Columbia, SC, Sunday, December 12, 1993, Page B1, "Trial Disclosed How Close Police Came to Catching Slippery Killer"

The Item, Sumter, SC, Saturday, December 17, 1994, Page 1, "Tucker Sentenced to Death"

Times and Democrat, Orangeburg, SC, Thursday, July 18, 1996, Page 1, "Convict's Use of Finding Religion as Defense Does Not Sway Decision by Calhoun Jury"

Times and Democrat, Orangeburg, SC, Sunday, May 23, 2004, Page 1, "Portrait of a Killer"

Gaffney Ledger, SC, Monday, May 31, 2004, Page 9, "Inmate Put to Death in Electric Chair" by Jeffrey Collins

About the Authors

Want to help out a couple of hard-working indie authors? Please leave a review on Amazon or Goodreads!

Scott Lunsford has 33 years of law enforcement experience. He has worked as a detective and supervisor in youth services, a school resource officer, and a patrol supervisor in Asheville, N.C. Scott is currently a school resource officer for the Madison County Sheriff's Office. He is also the host of the Felon File Podcast at felonfile.com. For more information about Scott and his work, visit scottlunsfordauthor.com.

Alfred Dockery is an award-winning writer and editor. A former trade press journalist, he has written for multiple publications, including Textile World and Furniture Today. In addition to his day job as a technical editor, he writes about historic true crimes on Medium and historically bad science and inventions on Substack: A History of Bad Ideas. Alfred is an Asheville native and an NC State graduate. You can find more of his work on his blog, blueridgetruecrime.com.

Made in the USA
Columbia, SC
20 February 2025

54124212R00109